COLLINS
DIY
GUIDE

REPAIRS &
IMPROVEMENTS

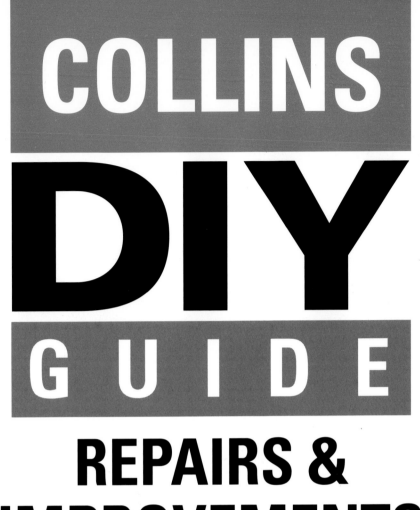

COLLINS
DIY
GUIDE

REPAIRS &
IMPROVEMENTS

JACKSON·DAY

HarperCollins*Publishers*

Published by
HarperCollins Publishers
London

This book was created exclusively
for HarperCollins Publishers by
Jackson Day Jennings Ltd
trading as Inklink.

Conceived, edited and designed
by Jackson Day Jennings Ltd
trading as Inklink.

Text
Albert Jackson
David Day

Editorial director
Albert Jackson

Text editors
Diana Volwes
Peter Leek

Executive art director
Simon Jennings

Design and art direction
Alan Marshall

Additional design
Amanda Allchin

Production assistant
Simon Pickford

Illustrations editor
David Day

Illustrators
Robin Harris
David Day

Additional illustrations
Brian Craker
Michael Parr
Brian Sayers

Photographers
David Day
Neil Waving
Shona Wood

Picture researchers
David Day
Anne-Marie Ehrlich
Hugh Olliff

Proofreaders
Mary Morton
Alison Turnball

For HarperCollins
Robin Wood – Managing Director
Polly Powell – Editorial Director
Bridget Scanlon – Production Manager

First published in 1988
This edition published in 1995
Reprinted 1996

Most of the text and illustrations in
this book were previously published in
Collins Complete DIY Manual

ISBN 0 00 412769 2

Copyright © 1988, 1995
HarperCollins Publishers

The CIP catalogue record for this
book is available from the British
Library

Text set in Univers Condensed
and Bodoni
by Inklink, London

Imagesetting by
TD Studio, London

Colour origination by
Colourscan, Singapore

Printed and bound
in Hong Kong

Please note
Great care has been taken to
ensure that the information
contained in this **COLLINS DIY
GUIDE** is accurate. However, the
law concerning Building
Regulations, planning, local
bylaws and related matters is
neither static nor simple. A book
of this nature cannot replace
specialist advice in appropriate
cases and therefore no
responsibility can be accepted by
the publishers or by the authors
for any loss or damage caused by
reliance upon the accuracy of
such information.

Picture sources

Key to photographic credits
L = Left, R = Right, T = Top,
TL = Top left, TR = Top right,
C = Centre, UC = Upper centre,
LC = Lower centre, CL = Centre Left,
CR = Centre right, B = Bottom,
BL = Bottom left, BC = Bottom centre,
BR = Bottom right

David Day: 74
Howard Ceilings: 32
The Velux Company Ltd: 75
Neil Waving: 41, 54, 59
Shona Wood: 28

Cross-references
Since there are few DIY projects that do not require a combination of skills, you might have to refer to more than one section of this book. The list of cross-references in the margin will help you locate relevant sections or specific information related to the job in hand.

CONTENTS

BRICK HOUSE
CONSTRUCTION

Brick-built houses follow a long tradition of styles and methods of construction. The brickwork gives the building character and is the main loadbearing element. If you have to repair and renovate your home it is useful to understand the basic principles of its construction.

Support for the house

To support the weight of the structure, most brick-built buildings are supported on a solid base called foundations (see diagrams left).

Wall formation

External walls are loadbearing, supporting roof, floors and internal walls. Cavity walls comprise two leaves braced with metal ties; older houses have solid walls at least 225mm (9in) thick. Bricks are laid with mortar in overlapping bonding patterns to give the wall rigidity. A damp-proof course (DPC) just above ground level prevents moisture rising. Window and door openings are spanned above with rigid supporting beams called lintels.

Internal walls are either non-loadbearing divisions which are made from lightweight blocks, manufactured boards or timber studding, or loadbearing structures of brick or block.

Solid and timber floors

Ground floors are either solid concrete or suspended timber types. A damp-proof membrane (DPM) is laid between walls where a floor is concrete. With timber floors, sleeper walls of honeycomb brickwork are built on oversite concrete between the base brickwork; a timber sleeper plate rests on each wall and timber joists are supported on them. Their ends may be similarly supported, let into the brickwork or suspended on metal hangers. Floorboards are laid at right angles to joists. First-floor joists are supported by the masonry or hangers.

Pitched-roof construction

Pitched (sloping) roofs comprise angled rafters fixed to a ridge board, braced by purlins, struts and ties and fixed to wall plates bedded on top of the walls. Roofs are usually clad with slates or tiles to keep the rain out.

Foundations
The foundations carry the whole weight of the house. The type, size and depth are determined largely by the loadbearing properties of the subsoil.

Strip foundation
A continuous strip of concrete set well below ground.

Trench foundation
Similar to the strip type, but concrete fills the trench.

Raft foundation
A concrete slab covers the whole ground area.

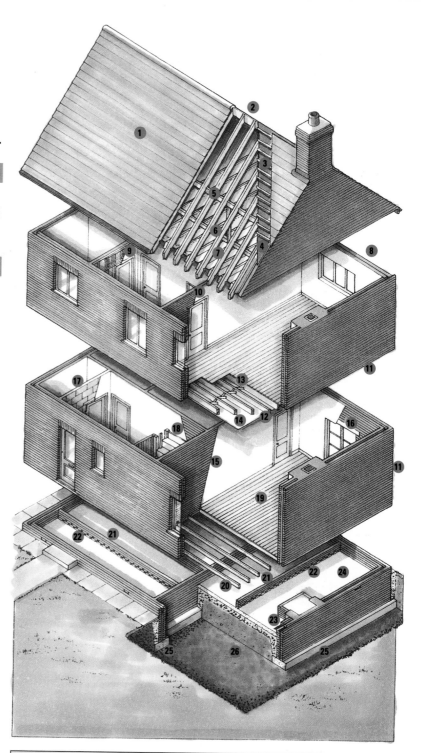

TYPICAL COMPONENTS OF A BRICK-BUILT HOUSE

1 Tiles or slates	9 Lath-and-plaster stud partition	15 Brick loadbearing internal wall	22 Sleeper wall
2 Ridge board	10 Internal brick wall	16 Lintel	23 Damp-proof course
3 Tile battens	11 Brick cavity wall	17 Block partition	24 Oversite concrete
4 Roofing felt	12 Suspended joists	18 Staircase	25 Strip foundation
5 Purlin	13 Herringbone bracing	19 Floorboards	26 Ground
6 Rafters	14 Plaster ceiling	20 Ground-floor joists	
7 Ceiling joists		21 Timber sleeper plate	
8 Wall plate			

TIMBER-FRAMED HOUSE CONSTRUCTION

SEE ALSO

Details for:	
Cavity walls	8
Floors	50-53

Timber is an excellent all-purpose material for building and has been used in house construction for centuries. Modern timber-framed houses differ from their brick-built counterparts in that the main structural elements are timber frames, irrespective of whether the walls of the building are clad with brickwork, timber boarding or tiles.

Foundations

A timber-framed house is built on sound concrete foundations. These are usually of 'strip' or 'raft' construction to spread weight to firm ground.

Wall assembly

Modern timber-framed house walls are constructed of vertical timber studs with horizontal top and bottom plates nailed to them. The frames, which are erected on a concrete slab or a suspended timber platform supported by cavity brick walls, are faced on the outside with plywood sheathing to stiffen the structure. Breather paper is fixed over the top to act as a moisture barrier. Insulation quilt is used between studs. Rigid timber lintels at openings carry the weight of the upper floor and roof.

Brick cladding is typically used to cover the exterior of the frame. It is attached to the frame with metal ties. Weatherboarding often replaces the brick cladding on upper floors.

Floor construction

Floors in a timber-framed house are either solid concrete or suspended timber, as with a masonry house. In some cases, a concrete floor may be screeded or surfaced with timber or chipboard flooring. Suspended timber floor joists are supported on wall plates and surfaced with chipboard.

Prefabricated roof

Timber-framed houses usually have trussed roofs — prefabricated triangulated frames which combine the rafters and ceiling joists — which are lifted into place and supported by the walls. The trusses are joined together with horizontal and diagonal ties. A ridge board is not fitted, nor are purlins required. Roofing felt, battens and tiling are applied in the usual way.

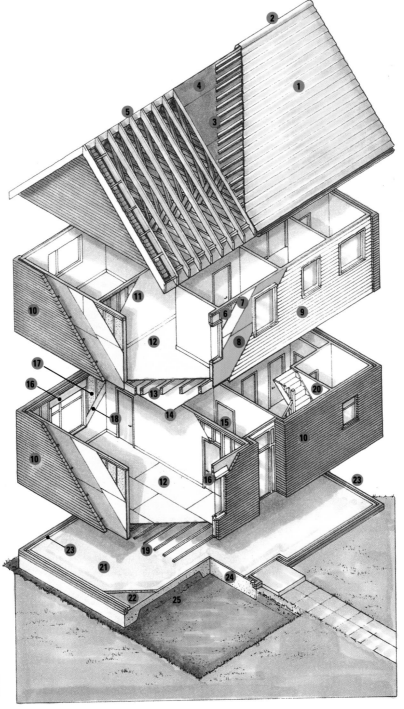

Foundation problems
Consult your Building Control Officer when dealing with problems or new work involving foundations.

Settlement
Settlement cracks in walls are not uncommon. If they have stabilized and are not too wide they are not a serious problem.

Subsidence
Subsidence caused by weak or shallow foundations or excessive moisture-loss from the ground can be more serious. Widening cracks from window or door openings are an indication of subsidence.

Heave
Weak foundations can also be damaged by ground swell, or 'heave'.

Light foundations
The walls of extensions or bays with lighter or shallower foundations than the house may show cracks where the two meet as a result of differential movement.

TYPICAL COMPONENTS OF A TIMBER-FRAMED HOUSE

1 Tiles or slates	8 Breather paper	15 Loadbearing internal stud wall	22 Damp-proof membrane
2 Ridge tiles	9 Weatherboarding	16 Lintel	23 Timber sole plate
3 Tile battens	10 Brick cladding	17 Insulation	24 Concrete slab
4 Roofing felt	11 Stud partition	18 Vapour barrier	25 Ground
5 Trussed rafters	12 Chipboard floor	19 Floor battens	
6 Timber-framed loadbearing wall	13 First-floor platform	20 Staircase	
7 Plywood sheathing	14 Plasterboard ceiling	21 Concrete screed	

WALLS:
EXTERNAL
WALLS

Solid walls provide good sound insulation but poor thermal insulation. There are three basic types, made from brick, block or natural stone. Cavity walls, a relatively modern form of construction, are more effective in preventing moisture penetration and heat loss than solid walls.

How solid walls are made

Solid walls are mainly constructed from bonded brickwork or concrete blocks, although local natural stone is also used in certain areas. They are usually at least 225mm (9in) thick — the length of a standard brick — but are frequently a brick and a half thick if they are to be exposed to severe weather conditions.

Moisture resistance
Moisture is prevented from penetrating to the inside surface of the wall by evaporation; rainwater absorbed by the bricks is normally drawn out before it reaches the inner surface. Moisture is prevented from being absorbed from the ground by an impervious damp-proof course (DPC), usually of bituminous felt, set in a bed joint of the brickwork at least 150mm (6in) — two brick courses — from ground level.

Weatherproofing qualities
Many solid walls are cement-rendered or otherwise clad to weatherproof the brickwork. Exterior-grade concrete blocks 225mm (9in) thick can be left exposed, but their appearance is improved by rendering. Natural stone walls are usually left bare and weatherproofing relies solely on the thickness and density of the material.

Solid walls
Traditional brick and stone walls will vary in thickness according to the age and size of the building. Concrete blocks are now common.

 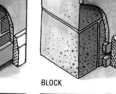 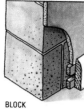

BRICK   BLOCK   STONE

Cavity walls
These have replaced solid walls in modern houses. A combination of brick, block and timber frame may be used to construct a cavity wall; brick is usually used for the outer leaf.

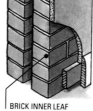 

BRICK INNER LEAF   BLOCK INNER LEAF   TIMBER INNER LEAF

How cavity walls are made

Typical cavity walls consist of two 100mm (4in) thick walls or 'leaves', separated by a 50mm (2in) gap. They may be constructed from bricks, concrete blocks, hollow clay bricks or timber framing, or a combination of these. The stretcher-bonded leaves must be tied together with metal wall ties (see left) to make them stable.

For the cavity to work as a moisture barrier, it is essential that the gap is not bridged. This can happen if mortar collects on the ties during construction.

Where openings occur at a doorway or window, the cavity is closed and a DPC is provided to stop moisture seeping in. Weep holes — unmortared vertical joints between every third or fourth brick — are usually provided in the outer leaf above lintels and below the main DPC. Their function is to drain any moisture from the cavity that penetrates the outer leaf.

Thermal-insulating panels are sometimes included as a cavity wall is built. Alternatively, the cavity is filled with an insulating material later on.

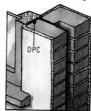   

Vertical DPC at window opening in cavity wall.

Weep holes are formed below main DPC.

Cavity ties
Cavity-wall ties are laid in the bed joints at 900mm (3ft) spacings horizontally and 450mm (1ft 6in) vertically. They are staggered on alternate brick courses.

Wire butterfly tie

Sheet-metal tie

IDENTIFYING LOADBEARING AND NON-LOADBEARING WALLS

The external walls of the house transmit the loads of suspended timber floors, most of the roof and other structures to the foundations. Usually all the external walls are loadbearing. The floor and ceiling joists and other internal walls might also be carried on loadbearing internal walls.

Not all internal walls are loadbearing, or 'structural'. Those that are can be identified by their position in the structure and the materials used in their construction.

A wall that carries the floor joists will have the floorboards running parallel with it. Check at each floor level, as a wall that passes through the centre of the house may carry the first floor but not the ground floor. Floor joists usually run in the direction of the shortest span. Check roof braces, which may bear on an internal wall.

Loadbearing walls are usually made of brick or loadbearing concrete blocks. Occasionally, wooden stud walls are used to carry some weight. A wall may also be termed loadbearing or structural where it is not actually carrying a load but is adding to the stability of the structure.

Non-loadbearing walls
Walls that divide the floor space into rooms and are not intended to support the structure are known as non-loadbearing. They may be made of brick, lightweight concrete blocks, timber studding or cellular-core wallboard, and are usually only a single storey in height. If the floorboards run under the wall it is likely that the wall is non-loadbearing.

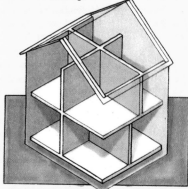

Non-loadbearing walls
These walls divide the internal space into smaller rooms and are relatively lightweight.

There are two types of internal wall: structural party walls, which divide houses built side by side, and partition walls, which divide up the space within a house and may be loadbearing or non-loadbearing.

Party wall construction

Party walls, or separating walls, are shared solid walls which divide houses built side by side. Party walls separate the properties over the entire height of the building to prevent the spread of fire and provide good sound insulation.

Partition walls

Internal partition walls can be loadbearing or non-loadbearing, but are usually relatively lightweight and not more than one brick thick. Partition walls for houses may be made from brick, concrete blocks, hollow clay blocks, timber framing or cellular-core wallboard (see below). A plaster finish is usually applied to brick or block walls for a smooth surface.

Stud-partition walls
Timber-framed partitions called stud walls are common in new and old houses. They are usually made from 100mm (4in) wide sawn softwood. The vertical timbers, called studs, are placed 400mm (1ft 4in) or 600mm (2ft) apart from centre to centre. Diagonal braces may be included for strength.

Laths – thin strips of wood nailed horizontally to the studs – are used as a key for plaster in old houses, although plasterboard has now replaced lath-and-plaster on this type of wall. Stud walls are usually non-loadbearing, but they can carry a lateral load.

Stud walls offer a convenient duct for running services such as wiring, but because of their hollow construction special fixings are required when attaching anything to the surface.

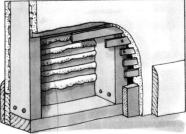

Lath-and-plaster stud partition

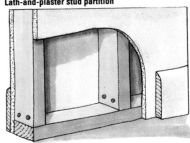

Plasterboarded stud partition

Lightweight concrete blocks
Blocks are widely used for modern partition walls. They are made to course with bricks and are nominally 150 to 225mm (6 to 9in) high and 450 or 600mm (1ft 6in or 2ft) long.

The most common size used is 450 x 225mm (1ft 6in x 9in) and a range of thicknesses from 50 to 300mm (2 to 12in) is available – use the 100mm (4in) wide block for a partition wall. This size corresponds to standard brick bonding, being equal to three courses high and two bricks long. Blocks are grey in colour and are made from cement and lightweight aggregate. Their large size makes building a wall quick and simple. They provide good sound and thermal insulation and are fireproof. Fixings can be made at any point on the wall using special plugs, and services can be channelled into the surface. Blocks are cut easily with a bolster chisel.

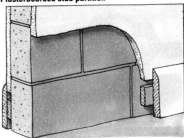

Plastered concrete-block partition

Hollow clay blocks
Clay blocks are red in colour, may be smooth-faced or horizontally grooved as a key for a plaster coating, and are hollow. They make a lightweight wall that has good sound and thermal insulation properties and is fireproof.

Hollow clay blocks do not take nails well; fixings should be made with screws and suitable cavity fixings. Where nailing is required – for fixing skirtings or door linings, for example – solid blocks should be incorporated.

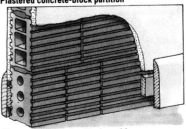

Plastered hollow clay-block partition

Cellular-core wallboard
This manufactured wall panel is made from two sheets of plasterboard with a gridded cardboard core bonded between them. It is available in similar sizes to standard plasterboard sheets, and 57 or 63mm (2¼ or 2½in) thick. The cell structure makes a light but rigid partitioning that is simple to install and can be decorated directly or finished with plaster. All fixings to this type of wall require a screwed cavity device unless wooden plugs are fitted during erection. The plugs are short lengths of the battening used to fix the panels together. It is necessary to preplan the placing of the fixtures before the plugs are driven into the core from the edge. The face of the board is marked to indicate the positions of the plugs before the partition is assembled. Clear channels for cable or pipe runs before beginning assembly.

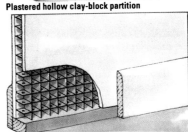

Cellular-core wallboard partition

Glass blocks
Hollow glass blocks can be used for non-loadbearing feature walls. Made in square and rectangular shapes and a range of surface patterns and colours, they can be either laid in mortar or dry-fixed. Get advice on methods of installation from your supplier.

SPANNING OPENINGS IN WALLS

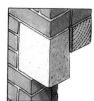
Stone and timber

Brick and steel

Reinforced concrete

Pressed steel

Rolled steel

TYPES OF LINTEL

A lintel bridges the gap above an opening. The type used will depend on the size of the opening and availability.

Wood
Wooden lintels were commonly built into the brick walls of older houses, often in exterior walls, behind a stone lintel or brick arch. They can suffer from rot due to penetrating damp, but are still used in timber-framed houses.

Brick
Brick lintels are used with wood, steel or concrete lintels over external openings, but are not strong. Some are supported by a flat or angled metal bar.

Stone
Stone is not strong in tension and cannot be used for wide spans. The stone lintels seen in older houses do not normally support the full thickness of the wall – timber lintels are used behind them.

Concrete
Concrete lintels are used for interior and exterior openings. Concrete is good in compression but not in tension. To overcome this, metal rods are embedded in the lower portion of the beam to reinforce it. Concrete lintels are made in a range of sizes to match brick and block courses and to suit various wall thicknesses. Though they are capable of spanning large openings, their weight can make handling awkward. Prestressed concrete lintels, reinforced with wire strands set in the concrete under tension, are lighter.

Steel
Galvanized pressed-steel lintels are widely used for internal and external openings. They are designed for cavity and solid walls of brick and block or timber-framed construction. The versions for cavity walls include a tray which channels moisture to the outside. Standard sections and lengths are available. They are fairly light in weight and some are perforated so they can be plastered direct.

Heavyweight rolled-steel joists (RSJs) are mainly used when making two rooms into one. The supplier will cut the I-section beam to length.

To create a doorway or window an opening must be made in the wall. In a loadbearing wall, the top of the opening must carry the structure above. Even cutting a hole in a partition necessitates propping the masonry.

Where supports are required

Doorframes and window frames are not designed to carry superimposed loads, so the load from floors above must be supported by a rigid beam called a lintel, which transmits the weight to the sides where the bearings are firm. Wider openings call for stronger beams, such as rolled-steel joists (RSJs). There are numerous beams, but all work in the same way.

The forces on a beam

When a load is placed at the centre of a beam supported at each end, the beam will bend. The lower portion is being stretched and is in 'tension'; the top portion is being squeezed and is in 'compression'. The beam is also subjected to 'shear' forces where the vertical load is trying to sever the beam at the points of support. A beam must be able to resist these forces. This is achieved by the correct choice of material and the depth of the beam in relation to the imposed load and the span of the opening.

Calculating lintel size

The purpose of a lintel is to form a straight bridge across an opening which can carry the load of the structure above it. The load may be relatively light, being no more than a number of brick or block courses, but it is more likely that other loads from upper floors and the roof will also bear on the lintel.

The lintel must be of suitable size for the job it has to do. The size should be derived from calculations based on the weight of the materials used in the construction of the building. Calculation for specifying a beam is, strictly speaking, a job for an architect or structural engineer. Tables relating to the weight of the materials are used to establish the figures.

In practice, for typical situations, a builder can use his experience to help you decide on the required size of lintel. A Building Control Officer may be happy to accept this type of specification, but he can insist that proper calculations are submitted with your application for Building Regulations approval.

When to support a wall

If you are creating a door, window or hatchway which is no wider than 900mm (3ft) across in a non-loadbearing wall, you can cut the hole without having to support the walling above provided the walling is properly bonded and sound. The only area of brickwork that is likely to collapse is roughly in the shape of a 45-degree triangle directly above the opening, leaving a self-supporting stepped arch of brickwork. This effect is known as self-corbelling. Do not rely on the self-corbelling effect to support the wall if you plan to make an opening which is more than 900mm (3ft) wide – provide temporary support for the wall as if it were loadbearing.

Before you make any opening in a loadbearing wall you will need to erect adjustable props as temporary supports, not only for the weight of the masonry but also for the loads that bear on it from floors, walls and roof above.

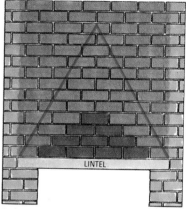

Self-corbelling
The darkest bricks are the only ones that may fall before the lintel is installed because of the self-corbelling effect of the bricks above. In theory the lintel supports the weight of materials within the 60-degree triangle plus any superimposed floor or roof loading, but when the side walls (piers) are narrow the load on the lintel is increased to encompass the area of the rectangle.

MAKING A HATCHWAY

RIGGING UP ADJUSTABLE PROPS

To remove part of a loadbearing wall it is necessary to provide support for the wall above the opening. Hire adjustable steel props and scaffold boards to spread the load across the floor. Where the brickwork will remain below the ceiling level, you will also need 'needles' to spread the load. Needles must be of sawn timber at least 150 x 100mm (6 x 4in) in section and about 1.8m (6ft) long.

For a hatchway or door opening, one needle and two props will suffice: place the needle centrally over the opening about 150mm (6in) above the lintel position. For wider openings, or where a load is great, space two needles and four props no more than 900mm (3ft) apart across the width of the opening.

Chop a hole in the wall for each needle and slot them through. Support each end with a prop, which works like a car jack. Stand the props on scaffold boards no more than 600mm (2ft) from each side of the wall.

A serving hatch is a convenient opening in a wall, usually between a kitchen and dining area, through which you can pass food, drinks and equipment. If you are blocking off a doorway, or making a stud wall, it may be advantageous to allow for a hatch. Alternatively, you may want to make a hatchway in an existing wall.

Planning the size and shape

Ideally, the bottom of the opening should be an extension of the kitchen worktop or at least flush with a work surface: 900mm (3ft) is a comfortable working height and the standard height for kitchen worktops. For practicality – for passing through a tray and serving dishes, for instance – it should not be narrower than 740mm (2ft 6in).

Hatches should be fitted with some means of closing the opening for privacy, for preventing cooking smells from drifting and, in some cases, so that they act as a fire-check (see right).

Creating the opening

You can make a hatchway in either a loadbearing or a solid non-loadbearing wall in much the same way: the main requirement with the former is temporary support for the masonry above and the load imposed on the wall. Mark the position for the hatch on the wall. Align the hole with the vertical and horizontal mortar courses between the bricks to save having to cut too many of the latter – hack off a square of plaster at the centre to locate the joints.

Drill through at the corners of the opening and mark out the shape and position of the hatch on the other side of the wall. Make the hole about 25mm (1in) oversize to allow for fitting a lining frame. Mark the lintel position.

Set up adjustable props and needles if you are working on a loadbearing wall (see left), then chop a slot for the lintel with a club hammer and bolster chisel on a brick wall this will probably be a single course of bricks deep; on a block wall, remove a whole course of blocks and fill the gap with bricks. Set the lintel in mortar trowelled on to the bearings. Use a spirit level to check that the lintel is perfectly horizontal – pack under it with pieces of slate if necessary. Replace any bricks above the lintel that have dropped. Leave for 24 hours to set, then remove the props and needles and hack away the masonry below.

Making a hatchway in a stud wall

Cutting an opening in a stud-partition wall is simpler than making one in a solid wall, but if the wall bears some weight you will need to support the floor or ceiling above with props, using planks to spread the load.

Mark out, then cut away the plasterboard or lath-and-plaster covering from each side to expose the studs. For a hatch the same width as the distance between the studs (up to 550mm/1ft 10in), just skew-nail a nogging between them at the top and bottom of the opening. If it is to be wider, make the opening span three studs. Cut away part of the middle stud at the height you want the hatch, allowing for a horizontal frame member at top and bottom. Make the framing from studding timber and cut to fit between the two studs on each side of the cut one. Fit and check for level.

Fitting a lining frame

Line the hatch opening with 25mm (1in) thick planed softwood joined at the corners with butt joints or bare-faced tongue-and-groove joints for a neater result. The frame can either finish flush with the plaster wall surface and be covered with an architrave, or project beyond the plaster to form a lip or shelf.

The sides of the opening in a masonry wall are likely to be rough – it is not easy to chop a clean line. Make and fit the frame, then pack out the gap between masonry and lining with offcuts of wood. The frame must be truly square within the opening – check this with a spirit level before proceeding. Screw the frame to the masonry using fixing plugs, fitted when the frame is positioned. Make good with mortar all round it. Rake back the surface of the mortar and, when it has set, finish flush with plaster.

Solid walls
Locate joints before cutting the slot.

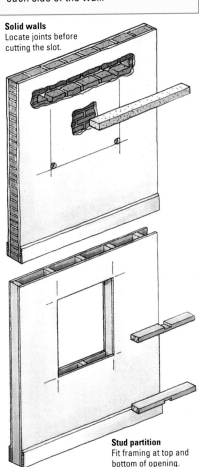

Stud partition
Fit framing at top and bottom of opening.

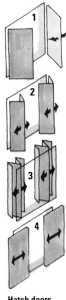

Hatch doors
1 Double-hinged
2 Twin bi-fold
3 Concertina
4 Horizontal-sliding

Finishing the frame
Use an architrave to cover the joint between the lining and wall or let the frame project to mask it.

Fit an architrave

Let frame project

11

CUTTING AN INTERNAL DOORWAY

1 Fix galvanized ties

2 Nail to wedges

Making a doorway in an existing wall may be necessary if you are changing the use of the room or improving its layout: this is often required as part of the process of converting a kitchen, where fitted units dictate the positions of access and exit doors. As with fitting a hatchway, it is necessary to install a lintel to ensure the stability of the wall itself and any other load which bears on it.

Preparing a brick or block wall

First check whether the wall is non-loadbearing or loadbearing. If the latter, seek approval from the Building Control Officer (BCO). Begin by marking the opening on one side of the wall, then examine the coursing of the bricks or blocks by exposing a small area; move the opening if necessary to align the perimeter with the vertical joints.

The height of the opening should allow for the height of the door plus 9mm (⅜in) tolerance, the thickness of the soffit lining and a new concrete or steel lintel. The width should be the width of the door plus 6mm (¼in) tolerance and twice the thickness of the door-jamb lining. Allow a further 12mm (½in) for fitting the lining.

Carefully prise off the skirtings from both sides of the wall. They can be cut and reused. Prop the wall and fit the lintel (see right) before cutting out the bulk of the masonry. Leave overnight for the bearings to set hard. The next day, starting from the top just below the lintel, chop out individual bricks, using a club hammer and bolster chisel. At the sides of the opening, cut the half or three-quarter bricks protruding into the doorway. Chop downwards where you can. If the wall is built from lightweight blocks, use a universal hand saw or a masonry saw to slice through the bonding. At the bottom, chop out the brickwork to just below floor level so that you can continue the flooring.

Bag up the rubble frequently in stout polyethylene sacks and stack whole bricks out of the way for reuse. Spray the area with water from a plant sprayer in order to settle the dust.

Fitting the door lining

You will have to fit a timber frame within the new doorway to which you can attach the stop-bead, door and decorative architrave. Make the frame from planed timber 25mm (1in) thick and the width of the wall. Fit the lining to the sides of the opening with galvanized-metal frame cramps (1) mortared into slots cut in the brickwork, or fit wooden wedges in the mortar joints and nail the frame to them (see diagram (2) left).

Dealing with a stud wall

First locate the positions of the studs, then prise off the skirting. Mark out the position for the opening on the wall, then remove the plasterwork. For lath-and-plaster walls, chop through to the laths with a bolster chisel and saw them off. For a plasterboard wall, saw through the cladding or use a sharp knife. If there are studs on each side of the opening, cut the plasterboard or laths flush with them. If the position of the hole does not correspond with the studs, cut back to the centre of the nearest stud on each side. Cut one or two studs to the right height – that is, the height of the door plus 9mm (⅜in) tolerance, the lining thickness and a 50mm (2in) head member.

Level up and and skew-nail the head member to the remaining studs at each end. Also dovetail-nail it to the ends of the cut studs. Saw through and remove the floor plate to the width of the door, plus 6mm (¼in) tolerance and twice the thickness of the door lining. Cut and nail the new studs, which will form the door jambs, to fit between the head and sill. Fit noggings between the new and original stud or studs. Cut and nail plasterboard to fill the gaps between the original wall surface and the new studs. Make and fit the door lining. Finish the surfaces with plaster, fit the architraves and replace the skirting.

Alternatively, cut the cladding from floor to ceiling and refit the studding flush with the cut edge. Mark the width of the opening, saw through the plaster from both sides of the wall then strip the plasterwork and knock out the exposed studs and noggings. Cut the floor sill level with the plaster and remove. Drive the studs into the cut edges until flush. Nail them at top and bottom. Fit a door-head member between them and a short vertical stud above it. Cover the space above the doorway with plasterboard.

INSTALLING THE LINTEL

Draw the position for the lintel, allowing a margin for fitting tolerance. Chop a groove around the perimeter of the opening with a club hammer and bolster chisel, then hack off the plaster. Fit adjustable metal props and needles, then cut a slot for the lintel. Bed a concrete lintel in a mortar mix of 1 part cement : 3 parts sand on bearings no narrower than 150mm (6in) at each side of the slot, and set level. Pack underneath the lintel with pieces of slate until it is horizontal. Replace loose bricks and fill any gaps with the same mortar mix.

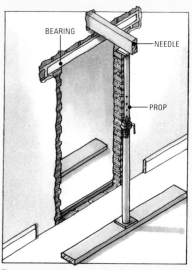

BEARING

NEEDLE

PROP

Fit a needle supported by props

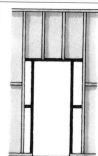

Door aligns with studs

Door is misaligned

Making the frame
The method you adopt for the frame will depend on the positions of the studs. The diagrams illustrate typical solutions.

Studs repositioned

FILLING AN OPENING IN A STUD PARTITION

Strip the door lining as described (see right). Trim the lath-and-plaster or plasterboard back to the centre line of the door-jamb studs and head member with a sharp trimming knife. Lever out the old nails with a claw hammer. Nail the new cut edge all round.

Nail a matching sill to the floor between the studs. Nail a new stud centrally between head and sill. Cut and nail noggings between the studs across the opening. Cut plasterboard 3mm (⅛in) less all round and fix to each face of the opening. Apply plaster or fill and tape the joints, then finish as required.

Nail the sill, stud and noggings

If you are making a new opening in a wall, you may also have to block off the original one. Obviously you will want the patch to be invisible, which takes careful plastering or filling of plasterboard joints.

Choosing the right materials

It is generally better to fill in the opening with the same materials used in the construction of the wall to prevent cracks forming due to movements in the structure (you can consider bricks and blocks to be the same). You could use a wooden stud frame with a plasterboard lining and plaster finish to fill an opening in a brick wall, but it would not have the same acoustic properties as a solid infill and cracks are difficult to prevent or disguise.

Removing the woodwork

Remove the architraves, then saw through the door-jamb linings close to the top and prise them away from the brickwork with a wrecking bar. If the linings were fitted before the flooring, the ends could be trapped: cut them flush with the floor. Next, prise the soffit board away from the top.

Bricking up the opening

Cut back the plaster about 150mm (6in) all round the opening. It need not be an even outline; unevenness helps to disguise the shape of the doorway.

To bond the new brickwork into the old, cut out a half-brick on each side of the opening at every fourth course, using a club hammer and bolster chisel. For a block wall, remove a quarter of a block from alternate courses.

It is not vital to tooth-in the infill if you are using blocks (which are easy and quick to lay) as it will require more cutting to fit. Instead, 100mm (4in) cut clasp nails driven dovetail fashion into the bed joints of the side brickwork (1) can be used to tie the masonry together.

Galvanized-metal frame cramps can also be used to save cutting into the bricks (2) – screw them to the wall, resting on every fourth brick.

Lay the bricks or blocks in mortar, following the original courses. If a wooden suspended floor runs through the opening, lay the bricks on a timber sole plate nailed across the opening. When the mortar has set, spread on a base coat of plaster, followed by a finishing coat. Fit two complete lengths of new matching skirting, or add to the original. When making up the skirting from old pieces, make sure the joints do not occur in the same place as the original opening.

1 Nail ties

2 Frame cramp

Cut out half-bricks

Lay bricks into the courses

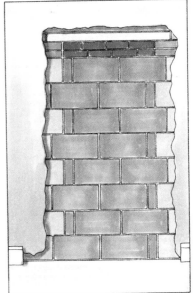

Cut blocks to match bonding

CONVERTING TWO ROOMS INTO ONE

Making a through room is the best way to improve access between areas frequently used – the dining and living rooms, for example – and provides an opportunity for redesigning your living space. The job uses similar principles to making a hatchway or a new doorway, although on a much larger scale. Removing a dividing wall – whether it is structural or simply a non-loadbearing partition – is a major undertaking, but it need not be daunting. Provided you follow some basic safety rules, much of the job is straightforward, if messy and disruptive. Before you start, plan out your requirements and consult the at-a-glance flow chart, right, for a break-down of just what is involved.

Do you want a through room?

Before you go ahead and demolish the wall between the two rooms, consider first just how the new space might function, its appearance, the time it will take you to carry out the work, and the cost you will incur.

Ask yourself the following questions: Will the shape and size of the new room suit your needs? (If you have a young family, remember that your needs are likely to change as they grow up.)

Will most of the family activities be carried out in the same room (eating, watching TV, playing music, reading, conversation, playing with toys, pursuing hobbies, doing homework)?

Will removing the wall deprive you of privacy within the family, or from passers-by in the street?

Will the new room feel like one unit and not a conversion? For example, do the skirtings and mouldings match? Are the fireplaces acceptable when seen together, or should one be removed? If the doorways are close together, should one be blocked off?

Will the loss of a wall make the furniture arrangements difficult – particularly if central-heating radiators are in use and take up valuable wall space elsewhere?

Will the heating and lighting need to be modified?

Will the proposed shape of the opening be in character with the room and of the right proportion?

● **Hiring professionals**
If in doubt, hire a professional builder: to save costs, you may be able to work as a labourer or do preparation and clearing work.

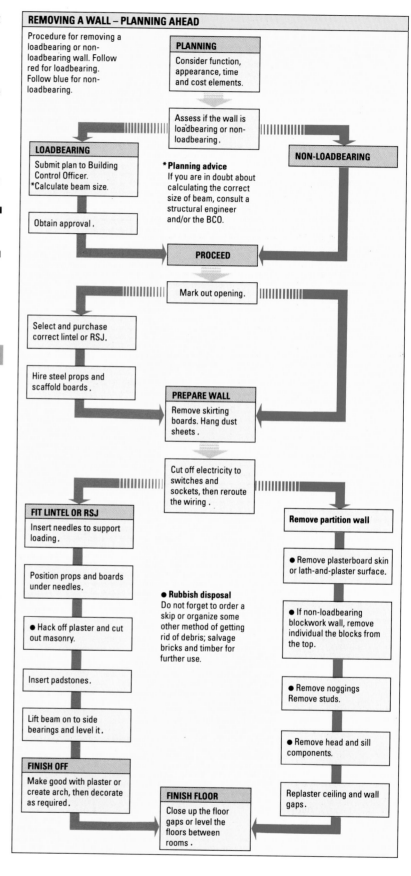

REMOVING A WALL – PLANNING AHEAD

Procedure for removing a loadbearing or non-loadbearing wall. Follow red for loadbearing. Follow blue for non-loadbearing.

PLANNING
Consider function, appearance, time and cost elements.

Assess if the wall is loadbearing or non-loadbearing.

LOADBEARING
Submit plan to Building Control Officer.
*Calculate beam size.

Obtain approval.

NON-LOADBEARING

* **Planning advice**
If you are in doubt about calculating the correct size of beam, consult a structural engineer and/or the BCO.

PROCEED

Mark out opening.

Select and purchase correct lintel or RSJ.

Hire steel props and scaffold boards.

PREPARE WALL
Remove skirting boards. Hang dust sheets.

Cut off electricity to switches and sockets, then reroute the wiring.

FIT LINTEL OR RSJ
Insert needles to support loading.

Position props and boards under needles.

● Hack off plaster and cut out masonry.

Insert padstones.

Lift beam on to side bearings and level it.

FINISH OFF
Make good with plaster or create arch, then decorate as required.

● **Rubbish disposal**
Do not forget to order a skip or organize some other method of getting rid of debris; salvage bricks and timber for further use.

Remove partition wall

● Remove plasterboard skin or lath-and-plaster surface.

● If non-loadbearing blockwork wall, remove individual the blocks from the top.

● Remove noggings Remove studs.

● Remove head and sill components.

Replaster ceiling and wall gaps.

FINISH FLOOR
Close up the floor gaps or level the floors between rooms.

SUPPORTING
A STRUCTURAL
WALL

Once you are satisfied that the opening will be an improvement to your home's layout, consider the practical problems. First, determine whether the wall is loadbearing or a non-loadbearing partition: bear in mind that a loadbearing wall will need a beam spanning the opening with at least 150mm (6in) bearings at each end. Mark out the proposed opening on the wall with chalk to help you visualize its size and proportion.

Choosing a beam

The most suitable beam is usually a rolled-steel joist (RSJ), although this type of beam will require preparation before it can be plastered over. Reinforced and prestressed concrete lintels can be used for openings up to about 3m (10ft) but, over a wide span, their weight makes them difficult to handle; prestressed types are lighter, but better for single door or hatch openings rather than wide spans. Pressed-steel box lintels – available in lengths up to 5.4m (about 18ft) – are lighter and can be plastered directly.

What size beam?
You can use the following rule of thumb for specifying an RSJ, although exact details depend on the location, and the result must be approved by the Building Control Officer. For pressed-steel lintels, refer to the manufacturer for sizes:

CALCULATING THE SIZE OF A BEAM

A rule-of-thumb guide used by builders.

Make beam 25mm (1in) deep for every 300mm (1ft) span.

Height of the opening

The height of the opening is to some extent determined by the height of the ceiling and the depth of the beam. The latter is determined by the width of the opening the beam has to span, and the load it must carry. Consult an architect or structural engineer who, for a fee, can calculate this for you. The beam can be positioned directly under the ceiling joists of a low ceiling.

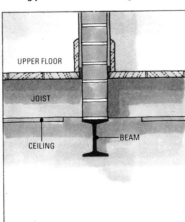

Brickwork supported below ceiling level

Brickwork supported directly under ceiling

Applying for permission

Before any work is started on a loadbearing wall you must seek approval from your local authority's Building Control Officer. He will require a drawing showing the proposed opening, its overall height and width and how the structure above the opening is to be supported. This need not be drawn up by a professional, but it should be clear. Approval is unlikely to be withheld provided the work complies with the Building Regulations. The BCO must be satisfied that the removal of the wall will not weaken the structure of the house, or any buildings attached to it, and that it will not encourage the spread of fire. Where a party wall is involved, it will be necessary to get written approval (a party award) from your neighbour. The BCO will advise you.

HOW A BEAM
IS SUPPORTED

The supports are usually brick piers, which are in effect columns attached to the side walls and formed from the remainder of the old wall. Concrete padstones are required on which to sit the beam. The BCO may want the piers increased in thickness to give sufficient support to the beam and the side walls.

Ideally, it would be better if no piers were used as they interrupt the line of the side walls running through. It might be possible to run the ends of the beam into the walls, eliminating the need for piers, but this is subject to Building Regulations approval. It requires a horizontal concrete beam called a spreader to be set in the wall and distribute the load across more of the wall.

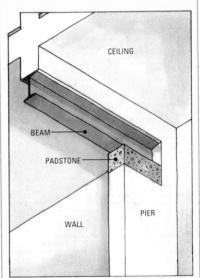

Pier capped by padstone supports the beam

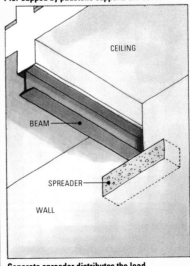

Concrete spreader distributes the load

REMOVING
THE WALL

Supporting the wall
1 When removing a wall up to ceiling level, support the upper floor with scaffold boards and props alone when the joists pass through the brickwork to support the wall. Otherwise, in addition, use needles on jacks placed directly above the props.
2 Normally brickwork projects below the ceiling level and is supported on needles passing through holes in the wall.

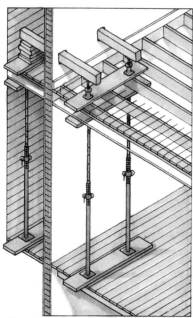

1 Layout for removing wall flush with ceiling

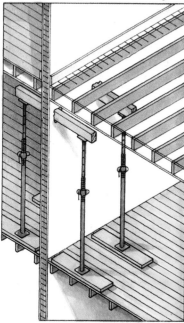

2 Layout for removing wall below ceiling

Props passing through the suspended floor

TRANSFER THE LOAD TO THE SUBFLOOR

If the floor appears to spring when you jump on it, check with a builder that the floor can carry the weight imposed; you may have to lift some floorboards and support the props on the foundations. In older houses, where there is no concrete below the floor, scaffold boards must be placed under the props to spread the load over the ground.

To remove part of a loadbearing wall you must temporarily support the walling above the opening. You will need to hire adjustable steel props and scaffold boards on which to support them. Where the beam is to be placed at ceiling level, hire extra boards to support the ceiling **(1)**. Generally you will have to fit needles through the wall to transfer the load to the props **(2)**. The needles must be at least 150 x 100mm (6 x 4in) in section.

Hire sufficient props to space them not more than 900mm (3ft) apart across the width of the opening. Buy the beam after the Building Control Officer's inspection. It can then be supplied to your exact requirements.

Preparation and marking out
First remove the skirting boards from both sides of the wall. On one side of the wall, mark the position of the beam in pencil. Use a steel tape measure, spirit level and straightedge for accuracy.

Hang dust sheets around the work area on the opposite face of the wall to help contain much of the inevitable airborne dust; attach them with battens nailed over them at the top. Seal gaps around all doors with masking tape to prevent the dust from travelling throughout the house. Open windows in the rooms you are working in.

Inserting the needles
Mark the positions for the needles on the wall, then cut away the plaster locally and chisel a hole through the brickwork at each point. Finish level

with the bottom of one course of bricks. Make the holes slightly oversize so you can easily pass the needles through. Position a pair of adjustable props under each needle not more than 600mm (2ft) from each side of the wall. Stand the props on scaffold boards in order to spread the load over the floor.

Adjust the props to take the weight of the structure and nail their base plates to the supporting boards to prevent them being dislodged.

Supporting the ceiling
If the ceiling needs supporting, stand the props on scaffold boards at each side of the wall and adjust them so they run virtually to ceiling height – they should be placed 600mm (2ft) from the wall. Place another plank on top of the pairs of props and adjust simultaneously until the ceiling joists are supported.

Removing the wall
Hack off the plaster using a club hammer and bolster chisel, then start to cut out the brickwork, working from the top. Once you have removed four or five courses, cut the bricks at the side of the opening. Chop downwards with the bolster pointing in towards the wall to cut the bricks cleanly. Remove all the brickwork down to one course below the floorboards. As you work, load the rubble into stout polyethylene sacks; it may be worth hiring a skip. The job is laborious, but you can make it easier by using a hired power brick-cutting saw (see below). Only use this method if you have experience with machine tools.

Cutting the opening
1 Remove or cut back the skirting and mark the beam's position.
2 Hang dust sheets around the work area.
3 Cut openings and insert needles.
4 Stand props on scaffold boards and adjust them to support the needles.
5 Cut away the plaster, then chisel out the bricks starting from the top of the opening.

Brick-cutting saw
Use with great care, following the suppliers' instructions.

Building piers

If the wall you are removing is deemed unsuitable as a basis for the supporting piers, you have two other choices. Where the adjacent wall is double thickness you may be able to cut a hole to take the end of the beam, allowing the weight to be distributed to the existing foundation. If this is not possible, you will have to build new piers with their own foundations. The piers must be built below the floor on concrete padstones cast on hardcore; they must include a DPC – engineering bricks may suffice – and must themselves be bonded in single or double brick thickness and toothed at every fourth course into the brickwork of the adjoining wall. The BCO will tell you the size for the piers.

Installing the beam

Make two wooden forms or boxes from thick plywood or softwood and cast concrete padstones on which to bed the RSJ to the size required by the BCO. Mix the concrete to the proportions 1 part cement : 2 parts sand : 4 parts aggregate. When the concrete has set, bed the padstones in mortar at the top of each pier. A large padstone may be better cast *in situ*. Set up formwork at the required height on each side and check the level between the two.

Build a work platform by placing doubled-up scaffold boards between steady stepladders, or hire scaffold-tower sections. You will need help to lift the beam into position.

Apply mortar to the padstones, then lift and set the RSJ in place. Pack pieces of slate between the beam and the brickwork above to fill out the gap. Alternatively, 'dry-pack' the gap with a mortar mix of 1 part cement : 3 parts sand, which is just wet enough to bind it together. Work it well into the gap with a bricklaying trowel and compact it with a wooden batten and a hammer. Where the gap can take a whole brick or more, apply a bed of mortar and rebuild the brickwork on top of the beam. Work the course between the needles so that when the timbers are removed the holes can be filled in to continue the bonding. Allow two days for the mortar to set, then remove the props and the needles and fill in the holes.

When the beam is fitted against ceiling joists you can use a different method. Support the ceiling with props and a board to spread the load (see opposite) on each side of the wall. Cut away the wall, then lift the beam into position and fit a pair of adjustable props under it. Apply mortar to the top of the beam and screw up the props to push it against the joists and brickwork above. Bed padstones in mortar or build formwork at each end and cast them.

FINISHING THE BEAM

A steel beam should be enclosed to provide protection from fire (which would cause it to distort) and to give a flat surface that can be decorated. Wet plaster, plasterboard or a specially made fireproof board can be used.

Cladding with plaster

Clad an RSJ with galvanized expanded-metal mesh to provide a key for the plaster. Fold the mesh around the beam, then lap it up on to the brickwork above and secure with galvanized nails.

Alternatively, wedge shaped wooden blocks (soldiers) into the recessed sides of the beam and nail the expanded metal to these. It is a good idea to prime the cut edges of the mesh to prevent corrosion which may stain the plaster.

Apply metal-lathing plaster or a stiff mix of bonding undercoat plaster in 9mm (⅜in) layers. Bond metal beading along the edges to reinforce the corners and cover with finishing plaster flush with the original surface.

Making good with plasterboard

To box in the beam with plasterboard or fireproof board you will need to fit shaped wooden blocks, wedged into the sides. To these, fix wooden battens nailed together to make fixings for the plasterboard panels (if you plan to install a folding-door system in the opening, you can nail the door lining directly to these same fixings). Set the board about 3mm (⅛in) below plaster level to allow for a skim coat to finish flush with the surrounding wall. Fill and seal the corner joints with tape.

Plaster the piers, then finish the beam and piers together.

● **Finishing a pressed-steel beam**
Pressed-steel box-profile beams are made with perforated faces to provide a key for the plaster.

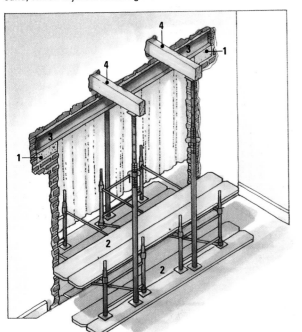

Installing the beam
1 Cast concrete padstones – set them on brickwork piers.
2 Set up a secure platform to enable two people to work safely.
3 Place the beam on the mortared padstones and check the level. Fill the gaps between the beam and the brickwork.
4 When set, remove the props and needles, then fill the holes.

Nail to brick

Tie with wire

Or nail to blocks

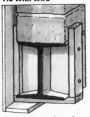

Or use plasterboard

17

FITTING ARCHES

Arch-formers
Expanded-metal mesh arch-formers are made in standard shapes and are easy to install. The shapes can be modified by adding a soffit strip.

Semi-circular

Oriental

Tudor

Spanish

Removing a dividing wall – to create a through living-and-dining room, for example – leaves you with a rectangular opening formed by the RSJ and its piers. If you prefer a curved archway, you can buy ready-made metal formers that are fitted in the opening and plastered over. Alternatively , design the archway yourself, construct your own formers and cover them with wet plaster or plasterboard.

Deciding on the arch profile

It is advisable to plan for the installation of an arch before you begin to make your opening. Choose the style of arch carefully: the shape will effectively lower the height of the opening at the sides, which may be impracticable and poorly proportioned for the room.

Corner arches round off the angle and do not encroach on headroom; semi-circular types give a full, rounded shape, but eat into headroom at the sides; pointed arches make a distinctive shape without taking up headroom at the middle of the opening.

Metal mesh arch-formers

Expanded-metal mesh arch-formers are available from builders' merchants. Various profiles are made – typically semi-circles, corner quadrants and ellipses, although Spanish, Oriental and Tudor styles are also available.

One-piece mesh frames are sold, but they are suitable only for walls 112mm (4½in) thick. Segmented formers – half the face and half the soffit (underside) – are more versatile; some have a separate soffit strip and can fit any wall.

Fitting the former
Wedge a batten across the top of the opening, to which you can attach the mesh with nails. Hold the former in position and set it squarely, using a spirit level (1). Secure the mesh to the piers with galvanized masonry nails – you may have to hack off a margin of plaster at the sides so the mesh can be fixed flat against the bricks. Hold a spirit level diagonally against the fold of mesh

at the curves and the hard plaster surface on the pier to check that it is set at the correct depth (2).

If you are fitting mesh segments, fit one half then the other (3) and tie the soffit strips together with galvanized or copper wire to prevent the mesh sagging under the weight of the plaster. On a thick wall, insert a soffit strip and tie it to the side pieces.

Mix up some metal-lathing plaster and spread a rough key coat on to the soffit with a plasterer's steel trowel, working from bottom to top from both sides (4). Do not press too hard or excess plaster will be forced through the mesh. Apply plaster to the face of the arch, scraping it off level with the hard plaster edge on the pier and the rigid mesh fold on the arch curve. When the plaster has stiffened, after about 15 minutes, apply a thin coat of ordinary finish plaster. Apply a second coat immediately and trowel smooth.

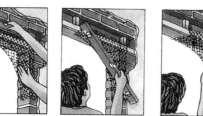

1 Set former square   **2 Check it is level**   **3 Tie former soffits**   **4 Apply plaster**

Fibrous-plaster arches

Prefabricated decorative archways made from fibrous plaster are available. These are normally fixed with screws to wooden battens at the top and sides of the opening. The joints between the fibrous-plaster mouldings and the wall

plaster are filled after installation. To complete an authentic-looking period interior, there are ornate fibrous-plaster accessories such as corbels (supporting brackets), pillars and pilasters with which to clad the piers.

MAKING A CUSTOMIZED ARCH

If you cannot find an arch former in the profile you require, make your own in one of two ways.

Using wet plaster
The arch may be a single curve, or it may incorporate intricate curves and points. Cut 12mm (½in) plywood ribs to the contour of the arch shape, but make them 12mm (½in) less than the finished size. Nail or screw them to the beam fixings and piers. Nail softwood spacer battens between the ribs.

Cut and fix expanded-metal mesh sheeting across the faces and edge of the shape, moulding it around the curves (1). You may have to snip the mesh with tinsnips to enable you to fold it around tight shapes.

Make up plastering guides from hardboard. Cut these to the finished shape you require. Temporarily nail them, smooth side inwards, over the mesh with packing pieces behind. The packing should equal the finished thickness of the plaster. Set the edges of the guide to overlap the underside of the arch by 12mm (½in), the required thickness of plaster. Spread plaster on to the underside of the arch between the overlapping edges. When this has set, remove the guides and plaster the wall faces, using the hard plaster edge as a level. Finally, apply finish plaster.

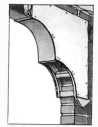

1 Fix mesh to ribs   **2 Fit plasterboard**

Using plasterboard
You can use plasterboard to make an arch to your own design. Cut the sheet to the required profile and nail it over the framework (2). Cut a thin strip of hardboard or thin plywood for the soffit, and pin it to the frame to form the underside of the arch. Fix hardboard textured side out. Bed paper scrim in plaster over the joins to prevent cracking due to slight movement. Apply a skim coat of finish plaster to all the surfaces. Alternatively, pin a strip of metal mesh to the soffit and apply a base coat and finish coat of plaster.

REMOVING A NON-LOAD-BEARING WALL

Lightweight partition walls which are not loadbearing can be removed without consulting the authorities for approval, and without the need to add temporary supports. You must, however, be certain that the wall is in fact not structural, as some partitions do offer partial support.

Dismantling a stud partition

Remove the skirting boards from both sides of the wall, plus any picture-rail mouldings: it is a good idea to save these for possible reuse or repairs in the future. If any electrical switches or socket outlets are attached to the wall, they must be disconnected and the wiring rerouted before work begins.

Removing the plasterwork
Use a claw hammer or wrecking bar to hack off the plaster and laths or plasterboard covering the wall frame. Once the framework is stripped, remove the vertical studs. Bag up the debris and remove it.

Removing the framework
First knock away any nailed noggings from between the studs. If the studs are nailed to the head and sill, they can be knocked apart. If they are housed or mortised in place, saw through them (at an angle to prevent the saw jamming). If you make the cut close to the joint, you will be left with a handy length of reusable timber.

Prise off the head and sill members from the ceiling joists and floor. If the end studs are fixed to the walls, prise them away with a wrecking bar.

Finishing off
Replaster the gap left in the ceiling and walls; you may need to fit a narrow strip of plasterboard. Fit floorboarding to close the gap in the floor if the boards are not continuous.

Dismantling a blockwork wall

Partition walls are sometimes made using lightweight concrete blocks. To remove the wall, start to cut away the individual units from the top with a bolster chisel and club hammer. Work from the middle out towards the sides.

Chop off an area of plaster first so that you can locate the joints between blocks, then drive your chisel into these to lever them out.

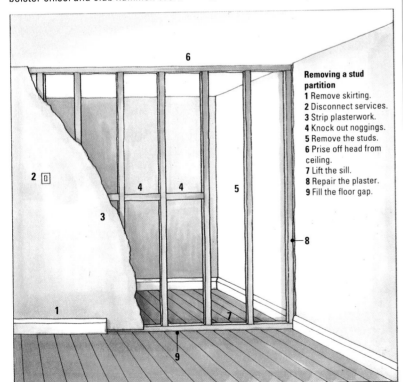

Removing a stud partition
1 Remove skirting.
2 Disconnect services.
3 Strip plasterwork.
4 Knock out noggings.
5 Remove the studs.
6 Prise off head from ceiling.
7 Lift the sill.
8 Repair the plaster.
9 Fill the floor gap.

METHODS OF CLOSING A FLOOR GAP

When you remove a dividing wall that penetrates the floor, you are left with a gap between the floors on each side. The floorboards may run parallel with, or at right angles to, the line of the wall. Filling the gap with new floorboards is straightforward.

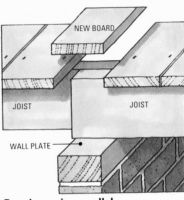

Boards running parallel
When the boards are parallel with the wall the supporting joists may rest on a wall plate built into the lower wall. Cut a board matching the thickness of the floorboards to fill the gap. Nail the board to the joist.

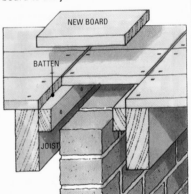

Boards at right angles
When the boards are at right angles to the gap, the ends will be supported on joists running parallel with the wall and about 50mm (2in) from it.

Cut the ends of the board flush with the joists. Nail 50 x 25mm (2 x 1in) sawn softwood battens to the sides of the joists, level with the underside of the boards. Cut short lengths of matching floorboards to bridge the gap and nail them to the batten.

● **Making a room divider in an old house**
Create a room divider by stripping the plasterwork from the studding to reveal the timber framework. Once it is clean, paint or stain the frame to suit your interior decorative scheme.

19

ALIGNING
FLOORS

When the joists run parallel with a wall that has been removed, you may find that one floor is not level with the other. This may have been caused by slight movement in parts of the building or it may be that the floors were never intended to be aligned. Depending on the difference between the floors, a slope or step will provide a satisfactory solution to the problem of misalignment.

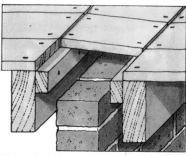
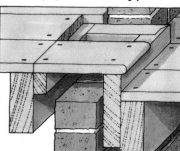

Fit short sloping boards across the gap

Packing and trimming

When the joists of the two floors are supported on the same wall plate, the chances are that both floors will be at the same level. Because wood can shrink or warp, however, it may be necessary to pack or trim the top of one or two joists slightly to allow for the infill board to sit properly between the floors.

Dealing with misalignment

A misalignment up to 18mm (¾in) can be accommodated by the short lengths of floorboards cut to span the gap. Although probably acceptable, the slope will be apparent. Where the difference in level is large, it may be necessary to create a single step or make a gradual slope. The latter should be less noticeable, but cannot satisfactorily run across a door opening.

Make a step if difference in level is large

Making a step

Trim the ends of the floorboards on the high side flush with the joists and nail a batten to it. Trim the boards on the low side in the same way, but screw a 38mm (1½in) thick planed softwood riser to the side of the joist to finish level with the batten on the higher floor (see right).

If the floors are to be covered, cut and nail short lengths of floorboards to form the step tread. Where you want a bare-wood floor, a single board running the width of the step would look better.

In this case, skew-nail noggings flush with and between the riser and adjacent joists at approximately 750mm (2ft 6in) centres – necessary for a wide board that is weak across its width.

Where a floor has been raised, make a shallow threshold step at a doorway. Prepare a hardwood threshold board to fit between the door linings and finish flush with the raised floor. Nail it to the lower floor. Trim the door to clear the step and refit it on its hinges.

Fit a threshold at a doorway

Making a gradual slope

Cut the floorboards flush with the joist on the high side, and nail a batten to the joist as before. Remove the skirting boards from the side walls and lift the floorboards from the room with the lowest floor. Rest one end of a stout straightedge on the batten nailed to the higher floor and the other end on one of the joists of the lower floor to make a gradual slope (**1**).

Take measurements between each joist and the underside of the straight-edge. Set an adjustable bevel to the angle between the side of each joist and the board. With a power saw, cut lengths of 50mm (2in) wide softwood at the required angle to fill these gaps. Nail the prepared packing to the tops of the joists in descending order (**2**).

Re-lay the floorboards, butting their ends against the boards of the higher floor. Insert new floorboards where necessary to fill any gaps.

For a finished-wood floor, re-lay and shuffle the boards from both floors to break up the straight joint line.

Replace the skirtings, following the line of the floor, and nail to the wall.

Setting the slope
Measure gap between a straightedge and each joist, and set an adjustable bevel to the angle. Cut packing strips to fit and nail in place, followed by the floorboards.

1 Use a straightedge to assess the slope

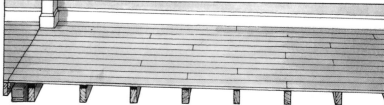

2 Nail packing to joists and relay floor

Building a partition to divide a large area into two smaller ones is quite straightforward to do, using a frame of timber studs. You can clad the wall and plaster it so the new addition looks an integral part of the house. Before you can go ahead, however, you may first need to seek approval from your local authority.

Complying with the Regulations

Before you begin to build a partition wall, check with your local authority to make sure that the space you are creating complies with the Regulations.

These state that if a new room is to be 'habitable' – a living room, dining room or bedroom (but not a WC, bathroom or kitchen) – it must meet requirements relating to ventilation.

The regulations stipulate that an open space must be available on the outside of the window to provide sufficient ventilation to the room. The openable area of the windows to each room must be not less than a twentieth of the room's floor area. (To check this, divide the area of the floor by the area of the window's sash or top vent.) Also, part, if not all, of the top vent must be 1.75m (5ft 9in) above the floor.

Alternative and additional means of ventilation may be provided by a mechanical ventilator direct to the open air. It may be permissible for a fanlight to connect to a vented lobby.

If you plan to partition a large bedroom to make an *en-suite* shower or WC on an internal wall, natural light will not be required, but ventilation will. Consider the positioning of the new room in relation to the existing plumbing and the means of ventilation.

Bear in mind the size and shape of the rooms in relation to the furniture – for example, should you plan to make a large bedroom into two smaller units, allow sufficient space for the beds to be made without difficulty. You will also need to create a corridor to make the two rooms self-contained.

Constructing a stud partition

Timber-framed non-loadbearing walls can be built relatively easily. The frame is usually made from 100 x 50mm (4 x 2in) or 75 x 50mm (3 x 2in) sawn softwood. The partition comprises a head or ceiling plate, which forms the top of the wall and is fixed to the ceiling joists; a matching length, nailed to the

floor, which forms the sill, or sole plate; studs which fit between the plates, equally spaced – about 400mm (1ft 4in) centre to centre – and fixed with nails; and short noggings which are nailed between the studs to make the structure rigid. Noggings are required where horizontal joints occur in the panelling.

Parts of a stud partition
1 Head plate
2 Sole plate (sill)
3 Wall stud
4 Studs
5 Noggings

Positioning the partition

If the new partition is to run at right angles to the floor and ceiling joists, it can be fitted at any point. Each joist will share the load and provide a solid fixing.

If the wall is to run parallel with the joists, it must stand directly over one of

them: this may mean altering the overall dimensions of your planned rooms. Locate the floor joist in question and check whether stiffening is required. If so, reinforce it by fixing an additional joist on each side (see right).

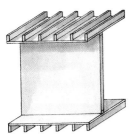

Right angle
A partition set at right angles to joists is well supported.

Parallel
A partition parallel with the joists must be supported by one of them.

Reinforcing
The floor joist may need stiffening to bear the extra weight of the partition (see right).

REINFORCING A JOIST

Remove the skirting and lift the floorboards. Temporarily lay some of the boards to walk on while working. Screw metal joist hangers to the walls at each end, using 50mm (2in) long screws, to support the reinforcing joists flush with the original joist. Cut two reinforcing joists to fit between the hangers. Allow not more than 6mm (¼in) for tolerance.

Use 12mm (½in) diameter coachbolts to clamp the joists together. Drill the holes for them slightly larger than their diameter and spaced not more than 900mm (3ft) apart, working from the centre. Place large plain washers under the head and nut.

Alternatively, you can use 75mm (3in) diameter double-sided timber connectors between the meeting faces instead of joist hangers. If you have room, and a drill bit long enough, drill through all three joists while they are held together with cramps. If not, clamp one in place and drill through the two. Remove the reinforcing joist and clamp the other on the opposite side. Drill through it using the hole in the original joist as a guide. Bolt the reinforcing joists together.

Replace the floorboards on which to erect the partition (see below).

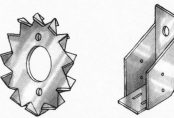

Timber connector   **Joist hanger**

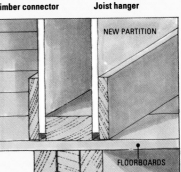

NEW PARTITION

FLOORBOARDS

CONNECTORS

COACHBOLT

REINFORCING JOIST

ORIGINAL JOIST

Stiffening the joist

Fitting a partition between joists
Fit timber bearers between the floor joists and ceiling joists to support the stud partition.

21

BUILDING A STUD PARTITION

Making a stud-partition wall is the easiest way to divide a room into two: you can construct a plain wall or add a doorway, serving hatch or glazed area to 'borrow' light from an existing window. You can build the partition directly on to the floorboards, or on to the joists below so that the flooring will be independent of the partition. The sides of the partition can be set against the plaster surface or set in channels to provide a better fixing to the masonry and make any unevenness easier to fill.

Marking out and spacing the studs

With chalk, mark the width of the sill for the new wall on the floor, using the sill member – a length of 100 x 50mm (4 x 2in) sawn softwood – as a guide to draw the line. Continue the guidelines up the walls at each side, using a spirit level and straightedge or a plumb line and bob. Make guidelines on the ceiling by snapping a distinct chalk line on to the surface with a taut string (1).

Spacing the studs
Lay the sill and head members together with their face sides uppermost. Mark the position of the studs at 400mm (1ft 4in) or 600mm (2ft) centres, working from the middle. Square the lines across both members, using a try square (2). Use the 400mm (1ft 4in) spacing to support thin board materials

and 9.5mm (⅜in) thick plasterboard, and the 600mm (2ft) spacing for 12.5mm (½in) plasterboard and tongue-and-groove (T&G) boards.

Marking out a doorway
If you require a doorway in the wall, make an allowance for the opening. The studs that form the sides of the opening must be spaced apart by the width of the door plus a 6mm (¼in) tolerance gap and the thickness of both door linings. Mark the width of the opening on the head plate, then mark the positions for the studs, working from the opening. Take the dimensions for the two sills from the head and cut both plates to length (3). The door studs overlap the ends of the sills, which must be cut back to allow for them.

Fixing the framework

Secure the sill to the floor on each side of the door opening, using 100mm (4in) long nails or 75mm (3in) long No10 countersunk woodscrews. Use the head plate as a guide to keep both parts of the sill in line. Prop the head plate against the ceiling on its line (4) and check the stud marks are true with the sill, using a plumb line. Nail or screw the head plate to the joists.

Measure the distance between the head and sill at each end and cut the outer wall studs to length: they should be a tight fit between the sill and head plate. Drill and plug the walls if you are fixing the studs with screws, or use 75mm (3in) long masonry nails.

Fixing door studs
Cut the door studs to fit between the

head plate and floor. Wedge them in place, but do not fix them yet. Add together the door height and the thickness of the head lining, plus 9mm (⅜in) for tolerance, then mark the position of the underside of the door head on the edge of one stud. Hold a spirit level on this mark and transfer it accurately to the other door stud.

Fixing the door head
Remove the studs, then mark and cut a 12mm (½in) deep housing to receive the 50mm (2in) door head. Reposition and skew-nail the door studs to the head plate and dovetail-nail into the ends of the sills. Locate the door-head member in its housing and dovetail-nail it through the studs (5). Fit a short stud between the head plate and door head.

Alternative fixing for door studs

An alternative method for fixing the door studs is to cut them to the required door height and double up with a stud between the sill and head plate. Support the door head and nail it to the top of the door studs. Cut a short length

of studding to fit vertically between the centre of the head plate and door head. Secure in place by dovetail-nailing. Make sure when nailing all the parts together that their faces are flush.

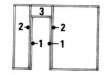

Double door studs
1 Door-height studs
2 Full-height studs
3 Door head

1 Snap a chalk line on the ceiling

2 Mark the sill and head plate together

3 Mark a door opening on the head plate first

4 Prop the head plate against the ceiling

5 Nail the studs to the door head

Fixing studs and noggings

Measure and cut each full-length stud and fix in turn (see right). Cut noggings to fit between the studs and, working from the wall, skew-nail the first end to the wall stud, then dovetail-nail through the next stud into the end of the nogging. One or two rows of noggings may be required: if you are going to fit plasterboard horizontally, place the centre of the noggings at 1.2m (4ft), working from the ceiling. When the boards are to be fitted vertically, space the line of noggings evenly, staggering them to make the fixing easier.

Space studs equally and nail top and bottom

Nail noggings between studs to stiffen them

Fixing to an existing stud wall

Stud partitions are commonly used for internal walls of rooms on the first-floor level. If your new partition meets a timber-framed wall, align it with the existing solid-frame members.

Where possible, fix the first stud of the new partition to one of the studs in the existing wall. Locate the stud by tapping, then drill a series of small holes through the plaster to find its centre.

When the new partition falls between studs, fix its first stud to the noggings, head and sill of the original wall. Construct the new wall as above but, in this instance, cut the wall stud to fit between the floor and the ceiling and fix it before the sill and head plate are nailed or screwed into place.

Fixing plasterboard vertically

Start at the doorway with the edge of the first board flush with the stud face. Before fixing, cut off a 25mm (1in) wide strip, running from the top edge of the board down to the bottom of the door-head member. Fix the board with 30mm (1¼in) or 40mm (1½in) plasterboard nails not more than 150mm (6in) apart. Fit the boards on both sides of the doorway, then cut and fit a section above the opening. Allow a 3mm (⅛in) gap at the cut joint. Fit the remaining boards.

Fixing plasterboard horizontally

Plasterboard can be fitted horizontally where it is more economical or convenient to do so. First nail the top line of boards in place, so that if it is necessary to cut the bottom run of boards the cut edge will fall behind the skirting. Cut a strip from the edge of the boards on each side of the doorway to allow for the boarding over the door to be fixed to the studs.

Temporarily nail a horizontal support batten to the studs 3mm (⅛in) below the centre line of the noggings. Sit a board on the batten and nail it to the studs. Fit the remainder of the top boards in this way; then fit the bottom row. Stagger the vertical joints.

A second person should assist you by holding the plasterboard steady. If you have to work alone, use a length of timber to prop the board while you work. Nail from the centre of the board.

NAILING TECHNIQUES

Use two 100mm (4in) round wire nails to skew-nail each butt joint, driving one through each side. Temporarily nail a batten behind the stud to prevent it moving sideways when you are driving in the first nail. Battens cut to fit between each stud can be permanently nailed in place to form housings for extra support.

Alternative stud-fixing method
For a particularly rigid fixing, set the studs into 12mm (½in) deep housings notched into the head and sill plates before nailing them.

Skew-nailing
Skew-nail a butt joint with two nails.

Nailing technique
Support the stud with a block while driving the first nail.

Supporting joint
Battens fixed to each side brace the joint.

Housing joints
Housing joints ensure a true and rigid frame.

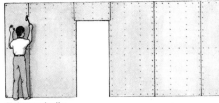
Fixing vertically
Work away from a doorway or start at one end.

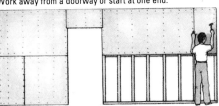
Fixing horizontally
Fix the top row first; stagger the joints on the next.

BUILDING
A STAGGERED
PARTITION

A stud wall can be built to divide a room into two and provide alcoves for storage at the same time. The method of construction is the same as described for the straight partition, but also includes right-angle junctions. Constructing a staggered partition with a door at one end and a spacious alcove, as shown below, makes sensible use of available space.

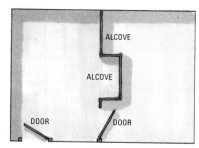

A staggered partition forms storage alcoves on each side, one for each room

Building the wall
1 Mark out partitions.
2 Transfer the marks to the ceiling.
3 Cut and fix the sills to the floor.
4 Fix the head plates to the ceiling.
5 Make corners from three studs.
6 Fix the other studs at required spacing.
7 Fit noggings, then fix the boarding.
8 Fit doorframe and complete the boarding.
9 Fit door lining, door and mouldings.

Positioning the wall

First mark out the thickness of the main partition across the floor, then mark the position of the 'recessed' partition parallel with it. For clothes storage, set them apart by 600mm (2ft).

Calculate the length of the partitions by setting them out on the floor. Starting from the wall adjacent to the doorway, measure off the thickness of a stud, the door lining, the width of the door, a second door lining and a second stud. Also add 6mm (¼in) for clearance around the door. This takes you to the face of the first short partition that runs parallel to the wall. Measure from this point to the other wall and divide the dimension in two. This gives you the line for the other short partition. Set out their thicknesses at right angles to the main partitions.

Fixing the sill and head plates

Mark the positions for the head plates on the ceiling. Use a straightedge and spirit level or a plumb line to ensure that the marks exactly correspond with those marked on the floor.

Cut and fix the sill and head plates to the floor and ceiling respectively, as for erecting a straight partition. Cut and fit the studs at the required spacing to suit the thickness of the cladding.

CONSTRUCTING THE CORNERS

The right-angled corners and the end of the short partition, which supports the doorframe, need extra studs to provide a fixing for the plasterboard. Make up a corner from three studs arranged and nailed in place. Fit short offcuts of studding to pack out the gap. Fix the offcuts level with the noggings. Fit the boards with one edge overlapping the end of the adjoining panel. For the end of the short partition, fit two studs 50mm (2in) apart with nailed offcuts between. Nail the board to the two faces of the partition. Leave the end exposed until the doorframe is fitted.

Measure and cut the door studs, head plate and door head to length. Nail the head plate to the ceiling, and fix one stud to the room wall and one to the stud wall. Ensure they are square and flush with the end of the partition. Fit the door head and a short vertical stud above it. Plasterboard above the doorway and to the side faces of the studs, including the end of the wall.

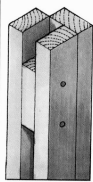

Corner post
Use three studs at the partition corners.

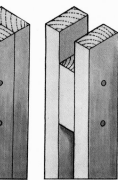

End post
Use two studs at the end of the partition.

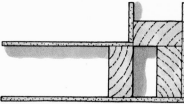

Overlap the plasterboard at corners

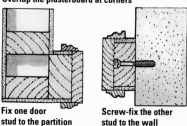

Fix one door stud to the partition

Screw-fix the other stud to the wall

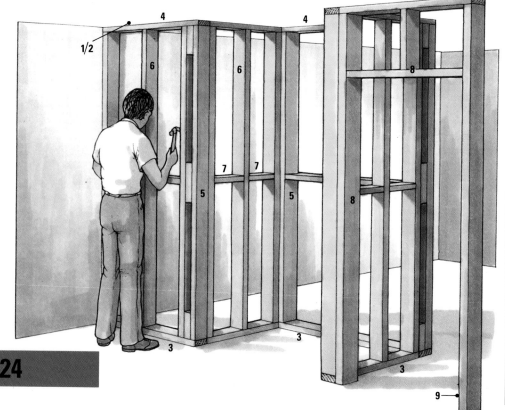

WALLS
CONSTRUCTING

FIXING TO
A STUD
PARTITION
SEE ALSO

Details for:	
Plumb line	76

Unlike solid walls of brick or block, stud walls are mainly hollow, presenting problems when wall fixtures are to be hung. Wherever possible these should be fixed directly to the structural stud members for maximum support, but if the positions of fixtures are preplanned, extra studding, noggings or mounting boards can be incorporated before the wall lining is applied.

Mounting a hand basin

A wall-mounted hand basin will need a sound enough fixing to carry its own weight and that of someone leaning on it when it is in use.

Buy the basin before building the wall – or work from the manufacturer's literature, which usually specifies the distance between centres for fixing the brackets – and position two studs to take the fixing screws. Mark the centre lines of the studs on the floor before applying the wall lining so that you can eventually transfer the marks to the face of the lining. Measure the height from the floor for the basin brackets and fix them securely with wood screws.

If you plan wall-mounted taps above the basin make a plywood mounting board to fit between a pair of standard-spaced studs to carry both the basin and the taps. Use exterior-grade plywood at least 18mm (¾in) thick. Plywood is tougher and more stable than softwood and chipboard does not hold screws well.

Screw 50 x 50mm (2 x 2in) battens to the inside faces of the studs, set back from their front edges by the thickness of the board. Cut the board to size with enough height to support basin and taps, then screw it to the battens to lie flush with the two studs.

Apply the lining to the side of the wall that will carry the basin, leaving the other side open for plumbing in the appliances. Drill clearance holes and fit the taps; fix the basin-support brackets, preferably with bolts.

To hide the plumbing within the wall, pass the waste downpipe through a hole drilled in the wall-sill member and run it under the floor. If the wastepipe must run sideways in the wall, notch the studs (see below).

Fitting a wall cupboard

It is not always possible to fix to the studs because walls tend to be put up well before furnishings are considered. If there are no studs just where you want them, you will have to use cavity fixings instead. Choose a type that will adequately support the cabinet.

Hanging shelving

Wall-mounted bookshelves have to carry a considerable weight and must be fixed securely, especially to stud partitions. Use a shelving system which has strong metal uprights into which adjustable brackets are slotted. The uprights spread the load across all the wall fixings. Screw into studs if you can, otherwise use suitable cavity fixings (see below right).

When the studs are spaced at 400mm (1ft 4in) centres, fix the shelving uprights to alternate studs. For 600mm (2ft) spaced studs fix to each in turn.

As an alternative, fix individual shelves along their back edges with extruded-aluminium shelf-supports screwed horizontally across the studs.

Hanging small fixtures

Load-carrying fixtures with a small contact area can crush the plaster and strain the fixings. Mount coat hooks, for example, on a board to spread the load and screw the boards to studs.

Hang small pictures on picture hooks secured with steel pins, larger ones on a double-pin type, preferably fixed to a stud. Use mirror plates fixed to the frame to screw a large mirror or picture to the wall. Suspend heavy frames from stranded wire, not twine.

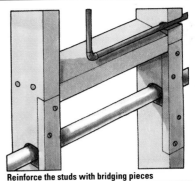

Mounting a basin
Fix a wall-mounted hand basin and taps to an exterior-grade plywood board.

FITTING SERVICES IN STUD PARTITIONS

It is easy to plan and fit services in a stud-partition wall before lining it. To guard against future occupants drilling into service runs, set horizontal cables or pipes no more than 150mm (6in) above floor level.

Plumbing
Plan the runs of pipes by marking the faces of the vertical studs or the noggings that brace them. Remember that a wastepipe must have a slight fall. When you are satisfied with the layout cut notches in the timbers for the pipework (see right).

Transfer the marked lines to the sides of the studs or noggings and drill holes for the pipes close to their front edges. Cut in to the holes to make notches. If cut at a slight angle they will hold the pipes while they are being fitted.

Notches cut for wastepipes must be reinforced to prevent them weakening the studs. Drill the holes in the centres of the studs, following the pipe run.

Before cutting in to the holes cut housings for 300mm (12in) lengths of 50 x 25mm (2 x1in) softwood to bridge the notches. Make the notches, set the wastepipe in place, then screw the bridging pieces into their housings flush with the fronts of the studs.

Noggings need not be braced, but fit one under a pipe bend as a support.

Running electric cable
Drill 12 to 18mm (½ to ¾in) holes at the centres of the studs for level runs of cable and in noggings for vertical runs. Fit extra noggings to carry mounting boxes for sockets and switches. For a flush-mounted fitting, inset the noggings to the depth of the box so that its front edge lies flush with the lining. Run the cable. With the lining in place, mark and cut an opening for the box and pull the cable through. If you have omitted a mounting board during construction, you can use dry-wall fixing flanges to hold the metal box to the lining.

Reinforce the studs with bridging pieces

Fit metal boxes to a mounting board

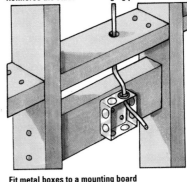

Spring-toggle fixing

Cavity fixings
Various cavity fixings are available for insertion into holes and securing with screws or bolts. Some expand to grip the lining as a screw is tightened; some are held in place by a toggle that springs out behind the lining.

25

BUILDING A
DRY-PARTITION
WALL

For a lightweight non-loadbearing partition, cellular-core dry-partitioning is easy to construct. Made from two sheets of plasterboard with a cardboard core, it makes a rigid wall when installed. The panels can be purchased from larger builders' merchants, but will probably have to be ordered. Tapered-edge panels for decorating and square-edged panels for plastering are available. The panels provide a reasonable level of sound insulation, but gaps between boards reduce their performance. Acoustic sealant can be applied to all the jointing surfaces during erection.

Fixing the framing

The panels are fixed to a lightweight timber frame. Mark out the floor, walls and ceiling in the same way as for a stud partition. Nail to the floor a 50mm (2in) planed (PAR) softwood sill, which matches the thickness of the partitioning. Plane 18mm (¾in) thick softwood ceiling and wall battens to make a snug fit in the gap between the plasterboard sheets. Remove the arris from the outside long edges of the battening and then nail or screw the battening to the wall and ceiling. To locate the bottom of the partition, cut a point on a 150mm (6in) locating block cut from wall battening, and nail it to the sill with its square end against the wall batten. Use 50mm (2in) wire nails.

Fixing the panels

Using a saw, cut the panels to fit between the sill and the ceiling with a 3mm (⅛in) tolerance . Rip out the cardboard core with the claw of a hammer to the depth of the battens – about 18mm (¾in) – along the top and two long edges. Also remove 150mm (6in) of the core from each end of the bottom edge. Use a wood chisel to trim away any lumps of glue.

Drive 150mm (6in) lengths of battening into the core at the bottom of the partitioning approximately 400mm (1ft 4in) apart. These plugs are used to fix skirtings. Mark the position of each plug on the surface of the partition for future reference.

Lift and locate the top of the first panel over the ceiling batten about 200mm (8in) from the wall. Swing the panel into the vertical position and locate it on the floor sill. Slide the panel carefully along the sill to locate over the locating block and wall batten. Cut an intermediate locating block 300mm (1ft) long and taper each end. Tap half of its length into the bottom corner of the panel's core and nail it to the sill.

Cut a length of square-section vertical joint batten to fit between the ceiling batten and intermediate locating block. Tap the batten halfway into the edge of the panel and then skew-nail it at the top and bottom. Fix the boards to the framework with galvanized nails at 225mm (9in) centres.

Prepare the other panels and secure them in the same way. Butt the edges of the tapered panels, but leave a 3mm (⅛in) gap between square-edged ones.

JOINTS AND JUNCTIONS

Joints
To make a T-joint, nail a vertical wall batten to one of the joint battens or to plugs cut from the joint battening and driven into the core of the corresponding partition. Fit the 150mm (6in) long plugs horizontally, about 600mm (2ft) apart, before erecting the partition. Hammer them into the edge, following a line of cells. Use a spare length of battening to drive the plugs further in if required. Always mark the position of the plugs on the surface.

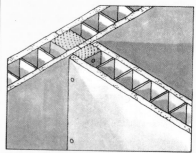

Fixing to joint batten

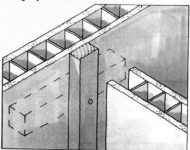

Fixing to batten plugs

Junctions
Right-angle corners are made by cutting away the inside face of the plasterboard and core to form a rebate for the full width of the adjoining panel. A batten must be fitted into each panel for nailing.

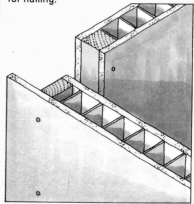

Right-angle corner assembly

Partition components
1 Softwood sill at base of panel.
2 Wall batten (hidden inside long edge of panel).
3 Ceiling batten.
4 Locating block (hidden).
5 Cellular-core panel.
6 Intermediate locating block.
7 Vertical joint batten.
8 Skirting-fixing plug.

Making a door opening

Mark the position of the doorway on the floor. Make allowances for the width of the door and door linings. Mark out the width of the panels, working from the opening to each wall. Fit the ceiling and wall battens. Cut the sill to stop at the opening and fix it to the floor. Fit the panels, working from the wall towards the opening and starting with any cut panels. At the opening, remove the core from the vertical edges of the panels and insert vertical battens flush with the edges. Skew-nail at top and bottom and fix the plasterboard with galvanized nails at 225mm (9in) intervals.

Measure and cut a panel to fit above the door opening. Nail a length of wall batten, with one end tapered, to the vertical batten on each side of the opening. The battens should be about 75mm (3in) shorter than the depth of the cut panel. Ensure they are set true.

Clear the core from all round the panel, allowing enough room at the bottom to accommodate a length of joint battening. Slide the panel over the side battens and nail it in place with a 3mm (⅛in) gap at the top.

Fit the horizontal head batten into the core, flush with the bottom edge, and nail it to the vertical battens at each end, then nail the door linings to the stud framework.

If you fit a ready-made doorframe, treat it as a panel and build it in as the other partitions are erected. When assembling the partition, remember to omit a section of the sill at the doorway.

Slide the panel over the side battens

Fitting a partition between walls

Working from one wall, mark out the width of the full panels across the floor. Inevitably, you will have to cut the last panel to fit. Measure and cut it to the required width, less 6mm (¼in). Fix the framing to the floor, ceiling and both walls. Fit the bottom locating batten.

Prepare and fit the cut panel at one end and then proceed from each end towards the centre. Clean out the core from the panels on each side of the opening to allow a jointing batten to be set in flush. Make three equally spaced wide saw cuts in the edges of the panels. Cut the vertical battens so that they fit loosely between the ceiling batten and sill. Set them flush into the prepared edges of the panel. Insert 50mm (2in) screws part way into the centre of the battens at each saw cut. Lift the last panel into position, then tap the screws sideways to drive half the vertical batten into the edge of it. Skew-nail the vertical batten to the top and bottom frames through the board. Fix the panels and remove the screws.

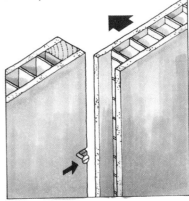

Insert last panel then tap batten sideways

Fixing details

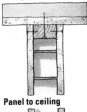

Panel to ceiling

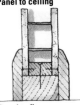

Panel to floor

Panel to wall

FITTING FIXTURES AND INSTALLING SERVICES

Fixtures
Lightweight loads such as pictures, small or medium-size mirrors, clocks and display shelving may be fitted to a dry-partition wall with cavity-wall fixings. Heavy loads, for example storage units, should be screwed to wooden plugs installed in the core before assembly. Shelving systems with metal uprights can be screwed directly to the plugs; a surface-mounted board screwed to a pair of plugs will help to spread the load of a heavy cabinet.

Services
Electric cable can be passed horizontally through the core as panels are erected. Use a 25mm (1in) diameter pipe to clear a path for the cable. A permanent length of plastic conduit running through the core may help you to feed the cable through as the panels are fitted. Vertical cable runs can also be made, provided they occur next to a joint in the panel and do not infringe Wiring Regulations.

Cut accurate openings in the face of the partitioning for switches and socket-mounting boxes, and fit them with partition-wall flanges.

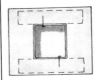

Mounting boxes
Plugs can also be employed for fixing mounting boxes in the core cavity.

Drive wooden plugs in from the edge

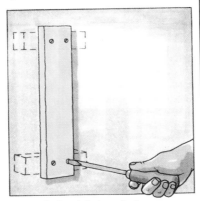

Fix mounting boards for heavy loads

CEILINGS: LOWERING A CEILING

From a practical point of view, a high ceiling can be a liability. It incurs greater heating bills, and decorating costs will be higher as more material is required to cover the walls. Lowering the ceiling can help solve these problems as well as providing a distinctive feature in a room.

High ceilings are generally found in older houses. Some are ornately moulded, while many have more simple yet attractive cornice mouldings. These should be preserved to maintain the character of the house, but where a room is plain and the ceiling needs attention, or where the proportions of the room would benefit from alteration, a lowered ceiling can be an improvement. It can be used to hide ducting, improve sound and heat insulation and provide a space for flush or concealed lights.

Changing the character of a room

A room's character is largely determined by the relation of its area to its ceiling height. Low cottage ceilings are considered charming and cosy, while tall rooms are felt to be very imposing when they are altogether large in scale. However, small rooms with high ceilings often feel rather 'uncomfortable'.

The sense of cosiness or otherwise may be based on practical experience. For example, a cottage room is smaller in volume than a room with the same floor area but with a higher ceiling, so it is easier to heat evenly – and a room with an even temperature feels more comfortable than one where the temperature varies due to rising and falling currents of air. Also, the acoustics in a small room may be better, inducing a relaxed atmosphere. Yet the qualities of light and space in a room are often due to a high ceiling, and if that were lowered, drastically changing the room's proportions, tall windows may look awkward and the sense of space be lost.

Making a model

Making a card model of a room is a good way to check that planned alterations will suit the room before you spend time and money on the real thing.

Measure the length, width and height of the room and the height, width and positions of the windows and doors. Mark out and cut rectangular pieces of

The lowered ceiling is sloped to accommodate the tall window

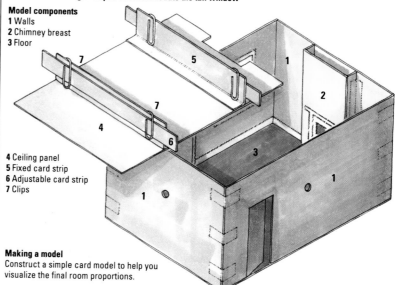

Model components
1 Walls
2 Chimney breast
3 Floor

4 Ceiling panel
5 Fixed card strip
6 Adjustable card strip
7 Clips

Making a model
Construct a simple card model to help you visualize the final room proportions.

stiff cardboard for the floor and walls to a scale of 1 : 10 (1mm = 1cm) or, in the imperial measure, 1 : 12 (1in = 1ft).

Mark the positions of the doors and windows on the cardboard walls and cut out the openings with a craft knife. Hinge a card door in its opening, using self-adhesive tape. Draw lines on the walls to represent the skirting and architraves around the doors and windows. You can colour these details to make them more realistic. Draw the fireplace to the same scale. If necessary, make a projecting chimney breast from card and glue it in place.

Punch a small peep-hole in each wall at a height scaled to the average eye level, and assemble the floor and walls, using glue or self-adhesive tape.

Cut a cardboard panel, representing the ceiling, to fit closely between the

walls. If the proposed ceiling is to be the suspended type, with lighting round its edges, cut the model ceiling panel smaller to provide the equivalent gaps at the sides of the room.

Cut two strips of card about 50mm (2in) wide and as long as the width of the ceiling piece, then glue them on edge across the back of the ceiling. Cut two strips a little longer, and use clips to attach these to the shorter ones. With the longer strips bridging the walls, adjust the paper clips to set the card ceiling at various heights. Check the effect on the room by viewing the interior space through the peepholes, and the door and window openings.

To simulate an illuminated grid-system ceiling, make a balsa-wood framework to the same scale and cover it with tracing paper.

Details for:
Making a hatch 33

You might want to lower a ceiling for practical reasons or simply to change the style of the interior – but whatever the reason, consider your options carefully because the outcome is liable to be expensive.

Timber-framed ceilings are heavy, but they can be tailor-made to suit the room, using basic wood-working skills.

Proprietary suspended-ceiling systems are relatively lightweight and particularly easy to install. Manufacturers offer a wide choice of materials for the panelling, but a strong grid pattern is unavoidable.

Use the chart (right) to help you consider a number of projects in advance and to compare one system with another.

PROJECT CONSIDERATIONS

Advantages of a lowered ceiling
- May improve room proportions.
- Provides a strong visual feature.
- Offers various lighting options.
- Conceals ducting.
- Reduces heating bills.
- Marginal saving on decorating materials.

Disadvantages of a lowered ceiling
- May spoil proportions of a room.
- Covers decorative plaster features.
- Large area can be expensive.
- Systems will require periodic cleaning.
- Some materials can be a fire hazard.

Points to check
- Recommended dimensions.
- Consult Fire Prevention Officer for kitchens.
- Style of proposed ceiling/interior.
- Ease of making.
- Cost of materials.
- Alternative systems.

Services
- New light fittings required. Surface, recessed and concealed types are options.
- Lighting circuit will need extending.
- May have to provide access for extractor ducting, electricity consumer unit, meter and water valves.

OPTIONS (see right)

LOWERED CEILING

Design features	Planning the scheme	Type of construction	Covering/finishes
Will change the room proportions. Will conceal old ceiling and services. Least likely to appear a conversion. Can be fitted with cornice mouldings. Without a hatch, it prevents access to the void above.	Make initial sketches of the proposed interior, then draw scale plans on graph paper to detail and cost the scheme. Make a scale model to visualize the effect of the ceiling.	This type of structure uses new ceiling joists that span the room in the shortest direction. The joists are notched over battens fixed to the walls. Ties and hangers are used for spans over 2.4m (8ft).	Materials: Plasterboard. Fire-resistant building board. Veneered board. Tongue-and-groove boarding. Mineral-fibre tiles. Finishes; papered, painted, varnished or ready-finished.

PART-LOWERED CEILING

Design features	Planning the scheme	Type of construction	Covering/finishes
Similar to the full lowered ceiling above, but has added interest in the form of a split-level. The end 'drop' can be vertical or sloped, the latter being preferable when it faces a window.	As for lowered ceiling (see above). Consider the line of the 'drop' in relation to a window. It should not cut across a window when viewed from the opposite side of the room.	Timber-frame construction as for lowered ceiling (see above). The end framework is formed from ties and hangers. The hangers are set at the required angle for a sloped end.	As for lowered ceiling (see above).

SLATTED CEILING

Design features	Planning the scheme	Type of construction	Covering/finishes
Not a true ceiling but a framework that appears to be continuous. It is most effective in a hallway or passage. It does not seal off the old ceiling. Can be dismantled for access to services.	As for lowered ceiling (see above). The spacing and depth of the slats can be varied: you should not be able to see between the slats when looking straight ahead.	Edge-on-plank construction using no sub-structure. Perimeter planks are housed and fixed to the wall; the slats are slotted into them.	No covering is used. The ceiling and walls above the slats are painted a dark colour. Finish for woodwork: light-coloured stain, clear varnish or paint.

SUSPENDED CEILING

Design features	Planning the scheme	Type of construction	Covering/finishes
As it is not attached to the walls, the ceiling appears to float in space: concealed lighting enhances this illusion. It is modern in character and masks old ceiling and services. Not demountable.	As for lowered ceiling (see above). Locate original ceiling joists and set out their position on your plan drawing: design the structure around them.	This is a timber-frame construction, using ties that are fixed to ceiling joists and carry hangers from which the new frame is suspended. The main components are bolted together.	As for lowered ceiling (see above).

SUSPENDED-CEILING SYSTEMS

Design features	Planning the scheme	Type of construction	Covering/finishes
A grid system manufactured from lightweight materials for self-assembly. Individual translucent or opaque panels sit in the grid framework. The system is demountable.	As for lowered ceiling (see above). Draw a plan of the room on graph paper and set out a symmetrical grid.	Lightweight aluminium T-section bearers are suspended from angle sections screwed to the walls. Bearers are loose-fitted.	Metal: anodized. Panel materials: plain, textured or coloured translucent plastic; opaque plastic; mineral fibre.

Vapour checks
Provide a vapour check to prevent condensation problems in an unventilated space above a lowered ceiling. Use a vapour-check plasterboard, an impervious sealer or polyethylene sheeting. The gaps between the boards or sheets of polyethylene must be sealed effectively.

Plasterboard
Bed joints in mastic

Polyethylene sheeting
Fold and staple edges

CONSTRUCTING A LOWERED CEILING

You can build a new ceiling at any practical height. However, the height of window openings may limit your choice. About 2.4m (8ft) is a useful height for a lowered ceiling; it is a common room height for modern houses and relates to standard wallboard sheet sizes. Most manufacturers of built-in furniture adopt it as a standard height for ceilings.

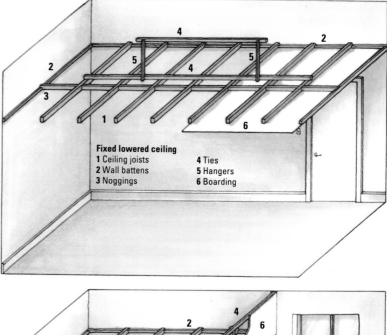

Fixed lowered ceiling
1 Ceiling joists
2 Wall battens
3 Noggings
4 Ties
5 Hangers
6 Boarding

Planning the layout

Making a lowered ceiling requires a considerable amount of timber for the framework and boarding to cover it. Work out your material requirements by drawing a plan to establish the most economical way to construct the ceiling. If you intend to use plasterboard, choose a vapour-check type. Arrange the panels with the paper-covered edges set at right angles to the timber supports. Stagger the end joints between each row of boards and arrange them so that they fall on a joist.

If you plan to use tongue-and-groove boarding buy it in lengths that can be cut economically to suit your joist arrangement, as short offcuts are wasteful. From time to time you will have to join boards end to end, using butt joints. Stagger short boards so that two adjacent joints do not coincide.

Materials for the framework

Make a cutting list of the materials you will need to make up the structure. Use 75 x 50mm (3 x 2in) sawn softwood for the ceiling joists. Calculate the number of joists you will need; they should span the room in the shortest direction and should be spaced at 400mm (1ft 4in) or 600mm (2ft) centres according to the thickness of the plasterboard. These dimensions are also suitable for other types of boarding.

You will need extra joist timber for the noggings fitted between the joists, plus 50 x 25mm (2 x 1in) sawn softwood for wall battens to run round the perimeter of the room.

Support spans of over 2.4m (8ft) with hangers and ties, made from timber not less than 50 x 50mm (2 x 2in) and fixed to the original ceiling above. Support the joists at about the middle of their span.

It is possible to use more hangers and reduce the section of the joists from 75 x 50mm (3 x 2in) to 50 x 50mm (2 x 2in). In this case place the hangers about 900mm (3ft) apart.

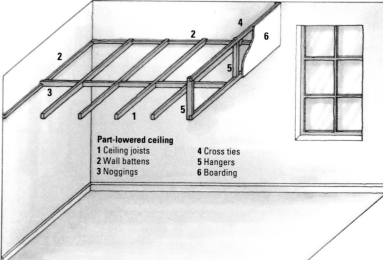

Part-lowered ceiling
1 Ceiling joists
2 Wall battens
3 Noggings
4 Cross ties
5 Hangers
6 Boarding

● **Cutting list**
A cutting list is your shopping guide. It will enable you to establish your requirements and help your supplier in making up your order. List the individual parts of the structure, and, under separate columns, fill in the quantity, length, width, thickness and material required.

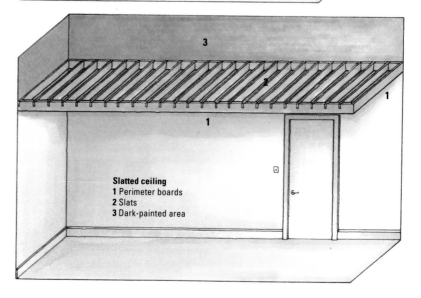

Slatted ceiling
1 Perimeter boards
2 Slats
3 Dark-painted area

Constructing the ceiling

Mark the height of the new ceiling, including the thickness of the boarding, on one wall. Draw a horizontal line across the wall at this level, using a straightedge and spirit level for accuracy. Continue the line around the room at this height. Cut the 50 x 25 mm (2 x 1in) wall battens to length. Nail or screw them to the walls at 400mm (1ft 4in) intervals, with the bottom edge level with the line.

Cut the 75 x 50mm (3 x 2in) ceiling joists to length. Notch the ends to sit over the wall battens to bring the bottom edges flush. Skew-nail the joists to the wall battens. Cut and fit hangers and ties to prevent long joists sagging (see opposite). These supports also stiffen the structure.

Cut and nail noggings between the joists to support the edges of the plasterboard. Nail tapered-edge plasterboard to the joists, noggings and wall battening. Fill and tape the joints between boards and walls.

Lowering part of a ceiling

You can lower part of a ceiling to overcome problems with tall window openings or to create a split-level effect. Follow the method for constructing a ceiling as described above, but enclose the end drop with plasterboard nailed to hangers suspended from a cross-tie member fixed above the last joist.

Making a slatted ceiling

Planed softwood planks 150 x 25mm (6 x 1in) in size, set on edge and spaced apart, can create a simple yet effective slatted ceiling. Smaller sections can be used where the span is short, as with a narrow hallway.

Cut four lengths of planking for the perimeter of the slatted ceiling. Before nailing or screwing them at the required height, mark and cut housings in two opposite planks. Space the housings 225mm (9in) apart. For boards less than 150mm (6in) wide, space the housings about 100 to 150mm (4 to 6in) apart. Cut notches in the ends of the 'slat' boards to sit in the housings so that the bottom edges finish flush.

Before fitting the slats, paint the walls and ceiling above the perimeter boards with a dark emulsion paint. Paint ducting or plumbing to disguise it. Finish the slats with varnish, stain or paint.

MAKING A SUSPENDED CEILING

A suspended ceiling is a framed panel that gives the impression that it is floating away from the walls. Fluorescent lights can be placed around the edge of the panel to enhance the floating effect and provide wall-washing illumination. Cover the panel with plasterboard, decorative veneered ply or mineral-fibre ceiling tiles.

Locate the position of the ceiling joists by noting the direction of the floorboards of the room above; the joists run at right angles to them. Pinpoint the joists from below by drilling pilot holes through the ceiling, then mark the centre of each joist.

Setting out the grid
Measure the lengths of the walls and draw a scaled plan of the room on graph paper. Set out the shape of the ceiling panel on the drawing with its edges approximately 200mm (8in) from each wall. Then set out the position of the 50 x 50mm (2 x 2in) softwood ceiling ties. The ties should run at right angles to the joists of the ceiling above. The ends of the ties and sides of the two outer ones should be about 300mm (1ft) from the walls. The number of ties you need depends on the size of the ceiling, but three should be a minimum. They should be spaced not more than 900mm (3ft) apart for adequate support.

Constructing the ceiling
Counterbore and securely screw the ties in position to each of the joists they cross. Cut 50 x 50mm (2 x 2in) softwood hangers to the required length and fix

them to the ties with coach bolts not more than 900mm (3ft) apart.

Cut additional ties to the same length as the planned ceiling panel. Bolt them across the ends of the hangers with an equal space at each end.

Cut the required number of 50 x 50mm (2 x 2in) planed softwood furring battens to suit the spacings necessary to support the boards or tiles used as a covering. Their length should be the span of the ceiling panel less two 50 x 25mm (2 x 1in) capping battens. Space the furring battens equally and screw them to the tie members. Counter-sink the screw heads.

Mark off the positions of the furring battens along the sides of each capping batten. Drive 50mm (2in) nails into, but not quite through, the cappings at these points. Apply woodworking adhesive and nail the cappings to the ends of the furring battens.

Finishing the assembly
Run electrical wiring for the fluorescent lights. Cover the underside of the frame with plasterboard, decorative veneered boarding or ceiling tiles. Fill and finish the surface and edges of a plasterboard ceiling panel. Finish the exposed edges of the frame to match the other materials as required.

Wire up slim fluorescent light fittings and fix them to loose boards that rest on top of the projecting frame. The light fittings can then be removed easily for servicing at any time. Provide enough spare electrical flex to allow the lights to be lifted clear.

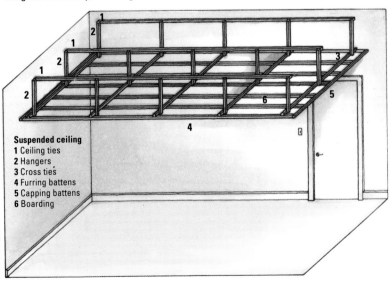

Suspended ceiling
1 Ceiling ties
2 Hangers
3 Cross ties
4 Furring battens
5 Capping battens
6 Boarding

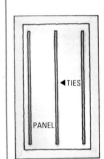

Setting out
Set out the panel on graph paper with a 200mm (8in) gap all round. Inset the ties about 300mm (1ft).

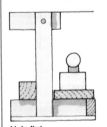

Light fitting
Fix a fluorescent light to a removable board for servicing.

31

SUSPENDED-CEILING SYSTEMS

SEE ALSO
Details for:
Levelling tools

Manufactured suspended-ceiling systems are made from slim metal sections, which provide a fairly lightweight structure for acoustic or translucent panels. They are quick and easy to fit and do not require specialist tools.

Manufactured systems
Manufacturers offer a choice of finishes for the framing as well as textured, translucent and opaque panels.

The lightweight alloy framework is made from three basic elements: an angle section, which is fixed to the walls; a main-bearer section, which spans the shortest direction; and a lighter T-section cross bearer, which bridges the space between the main bearers.

The loose panels sit on the flanges provided by the bearers. They can be lifted out easily to provide access to ducting or for servicing light fittings concealed behind them. You need at least 200mm (4in) above the framework in order to fit the panels.

Panel layouts

1 Main bearer centred

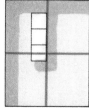

2 Panel on centre

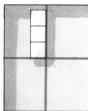

3 Cross bearer centred

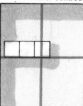

4 Panel on centre

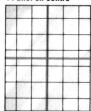

5 Best grid arrangement

Setting out the grid

Normally, 600mm (2ft) square panels are used for suspended-ceiling systems. Before fitting the framework, draw a plan of the ceiling on squared graph paper to ensure that the borders are symmetrical (see far left). Draw a plan of the room with two lines taken from the halfway point on each wall to bisect at the centre. Lay out the grid on your plan with a main bearer centred on the short bisecting line (1), then lay it out again with a line of panels centred on the same line (2). Use the grid that provides the widest border panels.

Plot the position of the cross bearers in the same way, using the other line (3,4). Try to get the border panels even on opposite sides of the room (5).

Fitting the framework

Before building a suspended ceiling with translucent panels, remove flaking materials and make good any cracks in the plaster ceiling above. Paint the ceiling with white emulsion to improve reflectivity if concealed fluorescent lighting is to be used.

Fix fluorescent light fittings to the joists, spacing them evenly across the ceiling: 16 watts per square metre is recommended for a suitable level of light in most rooms.

Mark the height of the suspended ceiling on the walls with a continuous levelled line. Hacksaw two lengths of angle section to fit the longest walls. Remove burrs from the ends with a file. Drill screw holes at 600mm (2ft) intervals. Drill and plug the walls, using the angle as a guide, and screw the components in place (1).

Next cut lengths of angle to fit the shorter walls. Their ends should fit on the angles already fitted. Screw-fix them in the same way.

Mark the positions of the bearers along two adjacent walls, as set out on the graph paper. Cut the main bearers to span the room. Sit them on the wall angles (2). Use a ceiling panel to check they are parallel and at right angles to the wall and each other. Cut the border cross bearers to fit between the end main bearers and wall angles. Set them in line with the points marked on the wall. Position the remainder of the cross bearers following the same line.

Working from the centre, drop in the full-size panels. Measure and cut the border panels to fit and then drop them into place.

Spanning wide rooms

If the size of the room is such that it exceeds the maximum length of the main bearer, join two or more pieces together. A joint-bridging piece is provided if the ends of the bearers are not made to lock together.

For spans exceeding 3m (10ft), support the main bearers with wire hangers. Fix each wire, spaced not more than 1.5m (5ft) apart, through a hole in the bearer and hang it from a screw eye in a furring strip or joist in the ceiling.

Lightweight suspended ceiling
1 Angle section
2 Main bearer
3 Cross bearer
4 Drop-in panels
5 Wire hangers

1 Screw the angle to the wall

2 Position the main bearers

INSTALLING A FOLDING LOFT LADDER

Access to the roof space is safer and more convenient if you install a folding loft ladder. Some are complete with built-in hatch cover, frame and fittings, ready to install in a new opening. Normally, the length of the ladders suits ceiling heights of 2.3 and 2.5m (7ft 6in and 8ft 3in), although some can extend to 2.9 to 3m (9ft 6in to 10ft).

Concertina ladder
To fix a concertina ladder, screw the fixing brackets of the ladder to the framework of the opening. Fit the retaining hook to the framework to hold the ladder in the stowed position. Operate the ladder with a pole that hooks over the bottom rail. Fit the hatch door to the frame with a continuous hinge and fix a push-to-release latch to the edge of the hatch door.

Ready-to-install folding ladder
Cut the opening and trim the joists to the size specified by the manufacturer. Insert the casing with built-in frame in the opening and screw it to the joists.

A concertina ladder is simple to install.

Folding ladders are easy to deploy.

Many houses have a hatch in the ceiling that provides access to the roof space for servicing water cisterns and maintaining the roof structure. Should your house have a large roof space without access, installing a hatch could provide you with extra room for storage. Although the procedure is basically straightforward, it does entail cutting away part of the roof structure.

In older houses this is not a problem as the timbers are substantial. In modern houses, however, lightweight timber is used to make strong triangulated trussed-roof structures. These are designed to carry the weight of the roof with each member playing an important part, so any alteration may weaken the structure. If your house is relatively new you should check with the company that built it, or with a local builder, that it is safe to proceed.

If you have a choice, site the hatch over a landing (although not too close to the stairs) so that lowering the access ladder will not cause disruption to the occupants, furniture or function of a room. Take into consideration the pitch of the roof, as you will need headroom above the hatch.

Making the opening
If you are planning to fit a special folding loft ladder, the size of the new opening will be specified by the manufacturer. In general, aim to cut no more than one ceiling joist: these are usually spaced 350mm (1ft 2in) apart.

Locate three joists by drilling pilot holes in the ceiling. Mark out a square for the opening between the two outer joists. Cut an inspection hole inside the marked area to check that there are no obstacles in the way of the cutting line. Saw through the ceiling plasterwork and strip it away.

Pass a light into the roof space and climb up into it between the joists. Lay a board across the joists to support yourself. Saw through the middle joist, cutting it back 50mm (2in) from each edge of the opening. Cut two new lengths of joist timber – called trimmers – to fit between the joists. Allow for a 12mm (½in) deep square housing at each end (1). Nail the housed joints, and the butt joints between the trimmers and joists. Use two 100mm (4in) round wire nails to secure each joint.

Nail the ceiling laths or plasterboard to the underside of the trimmers. Cut timber linings to cover the joists and the edges of the plaster. Make good the damaged edges of the plaster with filler. When set, nail mitred architrave moulding around the opening. Make a drop-in or hinged panel of 18mm (¾in) plywood or blockboard. If you plan to use the loft mainly for storage, fix chipboard panels over the joists. Cut the panels beforehand to ensure they will pass through the opening.

Alternative ways to install hatch covers

Drop-in recessed

Drop-in flush

Hinged up

Hinged down

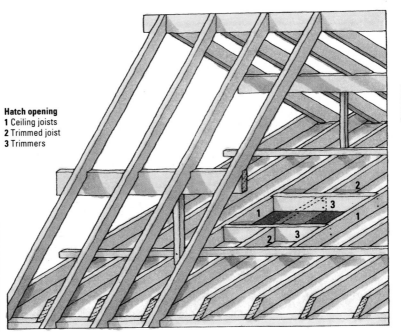

Hatch opening
1 Ceiling joists
2 Trimmed joist
3 Trimmers

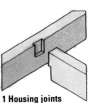

1 Housing joints
A housing joint will give better support to the trimmer joist than nails alone.

33

INTERIOR PLASTERWORK

Storing plaster
Keep an open bag of plaster in a plastic sack sealed with adhesive tape.

Plasterwork is used to provide internal walls and ceilings with a smooth, flat surface suitable for decorating with paint or paper. Plaster also provides sound and thermal insulation as well as protection from fire. Decorative mouldings – a feature of walls and ceilings in many older houses – are also made of plaster and are still available for renovations. There are basically two methods of providing a plaster finish: the traditional one is wet-plastering, while the modern method uses plasterboard and is known as 'dry-lining'.

Traditional plastering techniques

Traditional plastering uses a mix of plastering materials and water which is spread with a trowel over the rough background in one, two or even three layers and levelled accordingly. When set, the plaster forms an integral part of the wall or ceiling. The background may be masonry or timber-framed walls and ceilings finished with lath-and-plaster. Laths are thin strips of wood nailed to the timber framework to support plaster, which, forced between the laths, spreads to form nibs that grip on the other side. Traditional plastering takes practice before the plasterer can achieve a smooth, flat surface over a large area. With care, an amateur can produce satisfactory results, provided the right tools and plaster are employed and the work is divided into manageable sections. All-purpose one-coat plasters are now available to make traditional plastering easier for amateurs.

Dry-lining with plasterboard

Manufactured boards of paper-covered plaster are widely used to dry-line the walls and ceilings in modern homes and during renovations. Plasterboard obviates the drying-out period required for wet plasters and requires less skill to apply. The large, flat boards are nailed or bonded to walls and ceilings to provide a separate finishing layer. The surface may be decorated directly once the boards are sealed, or covered with a thin coat of finish plaster.

BUYING AND STORING PLASTER

Plaster powder is normally sold in 50kg (1cwt) paper sacks. Smaller sizes, including 2.5kg (5½lb) bags, are available from DIY stores for repair work. It is generally more economical to buy the larger sacks, but this depends on the scale of the work. Try to buy only as much plaster as you need – although it is better to overestimate to allow for wastage and to avoid running out of it at an inconvenient moment.

Store plaster in dry conditions. If it is to be kept in an outbuilding for some time, cover it with plastic sheeting to protect it from moisture. Keep the paper bags off a concrete floor by placing them on boards or plastic sheeting. Open bags are more likely to absorb moisture, which can shorten the setting time and weaken the plaster, so keep an opened bag in a plastic sack sealed with self-adhesive tape. Discard plaster which contains lumps.

Ready-to-use plaster is available in plastic tubs. It can be more expensive to buy, but it is easier for amateurs to use and will keep for a long time, provided the airtight lid is sealed well.

Traditional plastering
(Right)
The construction of a lath-and-plaster ceiling and plastered masonry wall.
1 Brick background
2 Ceiling joists
3 Lath background
4 Rendering coat
5 Floating coat
6 Finishing coat
7 Cornice moulding

Dry-lining
(Far right)
The construction of a modern dry-lined wall and ceiling.
1 Block background
2 Batten fixing
3 Ceiling joists
4 Noggings
5 Plasterboard
6 Coving
7 Tape
8 Filler

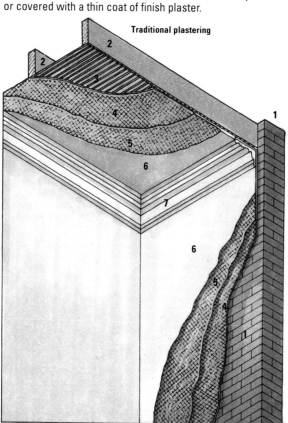

Traditional plastering

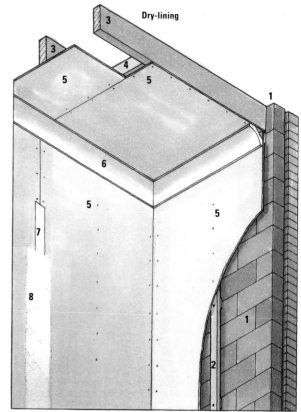

Dry-lining

TYPES OF PLASTER

SEE ALSO
Details for:
Applications   37

Plastering is carried out using modern gypsum plasters or mixes based on cement, lime and sand. By varying the process and introducing additives, a range of plasters can be produced within a given type to suit different background materials.

Plasters are basically produced in two grades – one as a base or 'floating' coat, the other for finishing coats. Base-coat gypsum plasters are premixed types which contain lightweight aggregates. Base-coat sanded plasters that are based on cement or cement/lime have to be mixed on site with a suitable grade of clean, sharp sand. Fine-powdered finish plasters only require the addition of water before they are ready to use.

The following information deals only with those materials that are suitable for domestic work.

CHOOSING PLASTERS FOR DOMESTIC WORK

Gypsum plasters
Most plasters in common use are produced from ground gypsum rock by a process that removes most of the moisture from the rock and results in a powder that sets hard when mixed with water. Setting times are controlled by the use of retarding additives which give each of the several types of plaster a setting time suitable to its purpose.

Gypsum plasters are intended for interior work only; they should not be used on permanently damp walls. They must not be remixed with water once they start to set.

Plaster of Paris
This quick-setting non-retarded gypsum plaster gives off heat as it sets. It is white or pinkish, and is mixed to a creamy consistency with clean water. It is unsuitable for general plastering, but good for casting, and can be used for repairs to decorative mouldings.

Carlite plaster
Carlite refers to a range of retarded gypsum plasters which are premixed with a lightweight aggregate and only need water adding to prepare them for use. The undercoat bonds well to most backgrounds, and this, coupled with their light weight – about half that of plasters mixed with sand – makes Carlite plasters fairly easy to use. The lightweight aggregate also gives some degree of thermal insulation. The average setting time for Carlite plasters is about two hours.

Four types of Carlite undercoat plasters – 'browning', 'browning HSB', 'bonding' and 'metal-lathing' – are available, each formulated to suit a background of a particular surface texture and suction. Browning is generally used for solid backgrounds with average suction (such as brickwork), while the higher impact-resistant HSB type is for high-suction backgrounds. Bonding undercoat is best for low-suction surfaces like dense brick or concrete blocks. Metal-lathing plaster is less commonly used and is primarily for an expanded-metal background.

When more than one undercoat layer is required to build up a thickness, the same plaster should be used for all layers to ensure compatibility.

There is only one Carlite finishing plaster; it can be used over all the undercoats, being applied as soon as the undercoat has set.

Thistle plasters
Thistle is the brand name of a range of building plasters used for a variety of conditions and backgrounds.

'Hardwall' is an undercoat plaster which provides superior impact and efflorescence resistance. It is suitable for most backgrounds.

There are two types of finishing plaster, both mixed with water only: multi-finish plaster, for use over sanded and hardwall undercoats, and board-finish plaster, used for finishing plasterboard surfaces.

Two special 'renovating' plasters are used on walls with residual dampness. The undercoat is a premixed gypsum plaster with special additives, and the finish plaster, formulated specially for use with the undercoat, contains a fungicide. These plasters are for damp walls that are slow to dry out, such as new exposed building work or in old houses where new damp-proof courses have been installed. This type of plaster is not itself a damp-proofing material, but it does allow the background material to breathe and dry out without letting the moisture show on the surface. Deal with the cause before you apply the plaster.

Sanded plasters
Before the advent of modern gypsums, lime and sand for undercoats and neat lime for finishes were employed in traditional wet plastering, often with animal hair added to the undercoat mix to act as a binder. Lime plasters are generally less strong than gypsum and cement-based plasters.

Lime is still used, but mainly as an additive to improve the workability of a sand-and-cement plaster or rendering. Cement-based sanded-plaster undercoats may be required by some authorities for kitchen and bathroom walls constructed on timber and expanded-metal lathing. These undercoats can also be used on old brickwork or where a strong impact-resistant covering is required.

Single-coat plasters
A universal one-coat plaster can, as its name implies, be used in a single application on a variety of backgrounds, and trowelled to a normal finish. The plaster is sold in 40kg (88lb) bags and only water need be added to prepare it for use. It will stay workable for up to an hour and some types can be built up to a thickness of 50mm (2in) in one coat.

One-coat plaster is also available in small packs, either ready-mixed or contained in mixing tubs. These are ideal for small repairs. For larger areas it is more economical to buy bigger bags and mix the plaster on a board in the usual way.

Ready-mixed plasters
A brush-on skim plaster is also available. It is applied up to 3mm (⅛in) thick with a wide brush, and smoothed with a spreader or trowel. When firm it is polished with a damp sponge.

Fillers
Fillers are fine plaster powders used for repairs. Some, reinforced with cellulose resin, are sold in small packs and need only mixing with clean water for use. They are non-shrinking, adhere well and are ideal for filling cracks and holes in plaster and wood.

● **Avoiding old plaster**
Plaster may deteriorate if stored for more than two months so suppliers try to ensure it is sold in rotation. The paper sacks in which plaster is supplied are usually date-stamped by the manufacturer. If you are buying from a self-service supplier, choose a sack with the latest date.

TYPES OF
SURFACE

● **Providing a 'key'**
Rake out mortar joints
to help plaster and
cement renderings
adhere to the surface.

A well-prepared background is the first step to successful plastering. New surfaces of block or brickwork may need only dampening or priming with a bonding agent, depending on their absorbency. Old plastered surfaces needing repair should be thoroughly checked. If the plaster has 'blown', hack it off back to sound material, then treat the surface and replaster the area.

Background preparation and absorbency

Brush down the surface of a masonry background to remove loose particles, dust and efflorescent salts. Test the absorption of the background by splashing on water; if it stays wet, consider the surface 'normal'. This means that it will only require light dampening with clean water prior to applying the plaster.

A dry background that absorbs the water immediately will take too much water from the plaster, making it difficult to work. It will also prevent the plaster from setting properly and may result in it cracking. Soak the masonry with clean water applied with a brush.

High-absorbency surfaces

For very absorbent surfaces, such as aerated concrete blocks, prime the background with 1 part PVA bonding agent : 5 parts clean water. When dry, apply a bonding coat of 3 parts bonding agent : 1 part water. Apply the plaster when the bonding coat is tacky.

Low-absorbency surfaces

Prime low-absorption smooth brickwork or concrete with a solution of 1 part bonding agent : 5 parts water. Allow to dry. Apply a second coat of 3 to 5 parts bonding agent : 1 part water, and trowel on the plaster when the bonding coat is tacky. Alternatively, allow it to dry for no more than 24 hours before plastering.

Non-absorbent surfaces

Glazed tiles and painted walls are considered non-absorbent and will require a coating of neat bonding agent to enable the plaster to stick. The plaster is applied while the agent is tacky. An alternative for glazed tiles is to apply a slurry of 2 parts sharp sand : 1 part cement mixed with a solution of 1 part bonding agent : 1 part water. Apply the slurry with a stiff-bristle brush to form a stippled coating. Allow to dry for 24 hours, then apply the plaster.

Another option is to chip off the old tiles, using a hammer and cold chisel.

Remove loose particles with a stiff brush

Prime porous surfaces to control the suction

A bonding agent improves adhesion

Smooth tiles can be 'keyed' with a slurry

MAKING FILLER
AND MORTAR BOARDS

Filler board
You can make a useful board for mixing and working with filler from 6mm (¼in) exterior-grade plywood. Cut out a 300mm (1ft) square with a projecting handle, or make a thumb hole as in an artist's palette. Seal the surface with a polyurethane varnish or apply a plastic laminate for a smooth finish.

Mortar board
Cut a piece of 12mm (½in) or 18mm (¾in) thick exterior-grade plywood, approximately 900mm (3ft) square. Round off the corners and chamfer the edges all round. Screw three lengths of 50 x 25mm (2 x 1in) softwood across the underside, spread equally apart. Make a 600mm (2ft) square 'spotboard' in a similar way.

Using a stand
You will find it easier to handle plaster with the mix at table height.

Using a stand
Use a stand to support the mortar board at table height, about 700mm (2ft 4in) from the ground. This enables the plaster to be picked up on a hawk by placing the latter under the edge of the board and drawing the plaster on to it.

Construct a folding stand, using 50 x 38mm (2 x 1½in) softwood for the legs and 75 x 25mm (3 x 1in) softwood for the rails. Make one leg frame to fit inside the other and bolt them securely together at the centre.

A portable Workmate bench can be used to support the mortar board instead of a stand: grip the centre batten in the vice jaws.

MIXING
PLASTER

SEE ALSO

Details for:
Builder's tools   76-77

With the background prepared, the next step is to make a good mix. It pays to mix your plaster close to the work site, as it can be a messy job. Cover the floor with plastic dust sheets or old newspapers, and remember to wipe your feet when leaving the room.

Plaster that is mixed to the correct consistency will be easier to apply. Use a plastic bucket to measure the cement, lime and sand or plaster accurately. For large quantities of plaster, simply multiply the number of bucket measures. For small quantities, just use half-bucket measures or less.

Old, hard gypsum plaster stuck to your equipment can shorten the setting time and reduce the strength of the newly mixed plaster. Do not try to rework plaster that has begun to set by adding more water: discard it and make a fresh batch. Mix only as much plaster as you will need. For larger areas, mix as much as you can apply in about 20 minutes – judge this by practice.

BONDING AGENTS

Bonding agents modify the suction of the background or improve the adhesion of the plaster. When you are using a bonding agent, do not apply the base-coat plaster any thicker than 9mm (⅜in) at a time. If you need to build up the thickness, scratch the surface to provide an extra key and allow at least 24 hours between coats.

Bonding agents can be mixed with plaster or sand and cement to fill cracks. Brush away any loose particles and then apply a solution of 1 part agent : 3 to 5 parts water with a brush.

Mix the plaster or sand and cement with 1 part bonding agent : 3 parts water to a stiff mix. Apply the filler with a trowel, pressing it well into the crack.

Wash tools and brushes thoroughly in clean water. It may be necessary to rinse out the brushes as the work progresses on a large job.

Wash agent from brushes before it sets

Undercoat plasters

Mix undercoat plasters on a mortar board (see opposite). For sanded plasters, measure out each of the materials and thoroughly dry-mix them with a shovel, or a trowel for small quantities. Make a well in the heaped plaster and pour in some clean water. Turn in the plaster, adding water to produce a thick, creamy consistency.

Just add water to premixed gypsum plasters (which already contain an aggregate). Mix them on the board in the same way. Always wash down the board after you have finished using it.

You can mix small quantities of premixed plaster in a bucket. Pour the plaster into the water and stir to a creamy consistency; 1kg (2lb 4oz) of plaster will need about 0.75 of a litre (1⅓ pints) of water.

Finish plaster

Mix finish plaster in a clean plastic bucket. Pour not more than 2 litres (4 pints) of water into the bucket, then sprinkle the plaster into the water and stir it with a stout length of wood until it reaches a thick, creamy consistency. Tip the plaster out on to a clean, damp mortar board ready for use. Wash the bucket out with clean water before the plaster sets in it.

PLASTER TYPES, APPLICATION AND COVERAGE

Type	Background	Type of coat	Coat thickness	Average coverage (m³ per 50kg) (sq yd per 50kg)
CARLITE				
Browning *Normal suction*	Brick walls	Undercoat	9mm (⅜in)	6.5–7.5 sq m (7¾–9 sq yd)
	Block walls	Undercoat	9mm (⅜in)	6.5–7.5 sq m (7¾–9 sq yd)
Browning HSB *High suction*	Concrete bricks	Undercoat	9mm (⅜in)	6.5–7.5 sq m (7¾–9 sq yd)
	Coarse concrete	Undercoat	9mm (⅜in)	6.5–7.5 sq m (7¾–9 sq yd)
Bonding *Low suction*	Brick walls	Undercoat	9mm (⅜in)	5.0–8.25 sq m (6–9¾ sq yd)
	Block walls	Undercoat	9mm (⅜in)	5.0–8.25 sq m (6–9¾ sq yd)
	Concrete bricks	Undercoat	9mm (⅜in)	5.0–8.25 sq m (6–9¾ sq yd)
	Smooth precast concrete	Undercoat	8mm (⁵⁄₁₆in)	5.0–8.25 sq m (6–9¾ sq yd)
	Plasterboards (Greyface)	Undercoat	8mm (⁵⁄₁₆in)	5.0–8.25 sq m (6–9¾ sq yd)
	Polystyrene	Undercoat	9mm (⅜in)	5.0–8.25 sq m (6–9¾ sq yd)
Metal-lathing	Expanded metal	Undercoat	9mm (⅜in)	3.0–3.5 sq m (3½–4 sq yd)
Finish	Carlite undercoats	Finish top coat	2mm (¹⁄₁₆in)	20.5–25.0 sq m (24½–30 sq yd)
THISTLE				
Hardwall	See Carlite undercoats	Undercoat	9mm (⅜in)	5.7 sq m (6¾ sq yd)
Multi-finish	Sanded undercoats	Top coat	2mm (¹⁄₁₆in)	17.5–22.5 sq m (21–27 sq yd)
Board-finish	Plasterboards (Greyface)	Top coat	5mm (³⁄₁₆in)	8.0–8.5 sq m (9½–10 sq yd)
Renovating *Normal suction*	Brick walls	Undercoat	9mm (⅜in)	6.0 sq m (7 sq yd)
	Block walls	Undercoat	9mm (⅜in)	6.0 sq m (7 sq yd)
	Concrete walls	Undercoat	9mm (⅜in)	6.0 sq m (7 sq yd)
Renovating-finish	Renovating plaster	Top coat	2mm (¹⁄₁₆in)	19.0–21.0 sq m (22¾–25 sq yd)
ONE COAT				
	All types	Undercoat/finish	12mm (½in)	4.5 sq.m. (5½ sq yd)

Plaster fillers

Pour out a small heap of cellulose filler on to a flat board or tile. Scrape a hollow in the centre with your filling knife and pour in water. Gradually drag the powder into the centre until it absorbs all the water, then stir the mix to a creamy thickness; if it seems too runny add a little more powder. Begin to fill deep holes and cracks with a stiff mix, but finish off with creamy filler.

APPLYING
PLASTER

Plastering can seem a daunting business to the beginner, yet it has only two basic requirements: that the plaster should stick well to its background and that it should be brought to a smooth, flat finish. Good preparation, the careful choice of plaster and use of the right tools should ensure good adhesion, but the ability to achieve the smooth, flat surface will come only after some practice. Most plasterer's tools are somewhat specialized, but their cost may prove economical in the long term if you are planning several jobs.

Problems to avoid

Uneven surfaces

Many amateurs tackle plastering with the idea of levelling the surface by rubbing it down when it has set. This approach is very dust-creating and laborious, and invariably produces a poor result. If a power sander is used the dust is unpleasant to work in and permeates other parts of the house, making more work. It is far better to try for a good surface as you put the plaster on, using wide-bladed tools to spread the material evenly. Ridges left by the corners of a trowel or filling knife can be carefully shaved down afterwards with the knife – not with abrasive paper.

When covering a large area with finishing plaster it is not always easy to see if the surface is flat as well as smooth. Look obliquely across the wall or shine a light across it from one side to detect any irregularities.

Crazing

Fine cracks in finished plaster may be due to a sand-and-cement undercoat still drying out and therefore shrinking. Such an undercoat must be fully dry before the plaster goes on, though if the plaster surface is sound the fine cracks can be wallpapered over.

Top coat and undercoat plaster can also crack if made to dry out too fast. Never heat plaster to dry it.

Loss of strength

Gypsum and cement set chemically when mixed with water. If they dry out before the set takes place they do not develop their full strength, and become friable. Should this happen you may have to strip the wall and replaster.

PLASTERING TECHNIQUES

Picking up

Hold the edge of the hawk below the mortar board and scrape a manageable amount of plaster on to the hawk, using the trowel (**1**). Take no more than a trowelful to start with.

Tip the hawk towards you and, in one movement, cut away about half of the plaster with the trowel, scraping and lifting it off the hawk and on to the face of the trowel (**2**).

 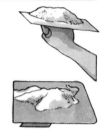

1 Load the hawk   **2 Lift the plaster**

Application

Hold the loaded trowel horizontally and tilted at an angle to the face of the wall (**1**). Apply the plaster with a vertical upward stroke, pressing firmly so that plaster is fed to the wall. Flatten the angle of the trowel as you go (**2**), but never let its whole face come into contact with the plaster as suction can pull it off the wall again.

1 Tilt the trowel   **2 Apply the plaster**

Levelling up

Build a slight extra thickness of plaster with the trowel, applying it as evenly as possible. Use a rule to level the surface, starting at the bottom of the wall, with the rule held against original plaster or wooden screeds nailed on at either side. Work the rule upwards while moving it from side to side, then lift it carefully away, taking the surplus with it. Fill in any hollows with more plaster from the trowel, then level the surface again. Allow the plaster to stiffen before you smooth it finally with the trowel.

Work the rule up the wall to level the surface

Finishing

Apply the finishing coat to a gypsum-plaster undercoat as soon as it is set. A cement-based sanded plaster must dry thoroughly, but dampen its surface to adjust suction before finish-plastering. The grey face of plasterboard is finished immediately without wetting.

Apply the finish with a plasterer's trowel, spreading it evenly no more than 2 to 3mm (1⁄16 to 1⁄8in) thick, judging this by eye. Plasterboard requires two coats to build a 5mm (3⁄16in) thickness.

As the plaster stiffens, brush or lightly spray it with water, then trowel the surface to consolidate it and produce a smooth matt finish. Avoid pressing hard and overworking the surface. Sponge off surplus water.

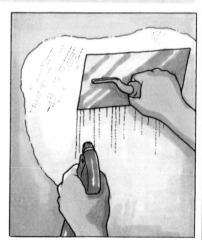

Spray plaster occasionally as you smooth it

The plastering of a complete wall is not likely to be required in many households. New work is more easily carried out with plasterboard, but there are times when repairs arising from problems with damp or resulting from alterations such as the moving of a doorway leave fairly large areas to be plastered. Plastering of this sort can be tackled by the non-professional, although some previous experience, such as patching up damaged plaster, would be an advantage. The key to success is to divide the wall into manageable areas.

Applying the plaster

Using the face of a plasterer's trowel, scrape a couple of trowel-loads of plaster on to the hawk and start undercoat-plastering at the top of the wall, holding the trowel at an angle to the face of the wall and applying the plaster with vertical strokes. Work from right to left if you are right-handed and vice versa if you are left-handed.

Using firm pressure to ensure good adhesion, apply a thin layer first and then follow this with more plaster, building up the required thickness. If the final thickness of the plaster needs to be greater than 9mm (⅜in), key the surface with a scratcher and let it set, then apply a second or 'floating' coat.

Fill the area between two screed battens. It is not necessary to work tight up against them. Level the surface with a rule laid across the battens, sliding the tool from side to side as you work from the bottom upwards. Fill in any hollows and then level the plaster again. Scratch the surface lightly to provide a key for the finishing coat and let the plaster set. Work along the entire wall in this way, then remove the battens. Fill the gaps left by the battens, again levelling the plaster with the rule.

With gypsum plasters the finishing coat can be applied as soon as the undercoat is set. Cement undercoats must be left to dry for at least 24 hours because of shrinkage, then wetted when the top coat is applied.

PREPARING TO PLASTER

In addition to specialized plasterer's tools, you need a spirit level and some lengths of 9mm (⅜in) thick planed softwood battening. The battens – known as screeds – are nailed to the wall to act as guides when it comes to levelling the plaster. Professional plasterers form 'plaster screeds' by applying bands of undercoat plaster to the required thickness. These can be laid vertically or horizontally.

Prepare the background and fix wooden screeds vertically to the wall with masonry nails. Driving the nails fully home will make it easier for you to work the trowel, but it can also make it more difficult to remove the screeds afterwards. The screens should be spaced no more than 600mm (2ft) apart. Use the spirit level to get them truly plumb, packing them out with strips of hardboard or wood as necessary.

Mix the undercoat plaster to a thick, creamy consistency and measure out two bucketfuls to begin with, though you can increase this to larger amounts when you become more proficient.

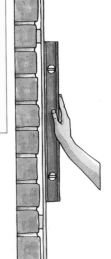

Plumb the screeds
Pack out the screed battens at the fixing points as required.

Finishing

Cover the undercoat with a thin layer of finishing plaster, working from top to bottom and from left to right (see left) using even, vertical strokes. If you are left-handed, work from right to left. Hold the trowel at a slight angle so that only one edge is touching.

Make sweeping horizontal strokes to level the surface further. You can try using the rule to get the initial surface even, but you may risk dragging the finish coat off. Use the trowel to smooth out any slight ripples.

Wet the trowel and work over the surface with firm pressure to consolidate the plaster. As it sets, trowel it to produce a smooth matt finish, but do not overwork it. Wipe away any plaster slurry which appears with a damp sponge.

The wall should be left to dry out for some weeks before decorating.

The order for applying plaster by a right-handed person

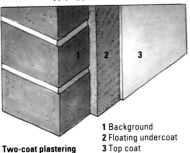

Two-coat plastering
1 Background
2 Floating undercoat
3 Top coat

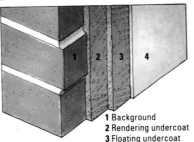

Three-coat plastering
1 Background
2 Rendering undercoat
3 Floating undercoat
4 Top coat

Plaster layers
Plaster is applied in layers to build up a smooth, level surface. Two or three coats may be used.

PLASTERBOARD

Plasterboard provides a relatively quick and simple method of cladding walls or ceilings and providing a smooth surface for decorating. It also offers good sound insulation as well as fire protection. It is quite easy to cut and to fix, either by bonding or by nailing it into place.

A range of dry-lining plasterboards is available from builders' merchants. The boards are all made with a core of aerated gypsum plaster and covered on both sides with a strong paper liner. A grey paper facing is for finishing with plaster while the ivory-coloured paper is for direct decorating with wallpaper or paint.

Plasterboard is made in a range of thicknesses and sheet sizes, usually with square or tapered edges. Tapered edges are invariably on the ivory-coloured side of a sheet (see below), whereas the edges on the grey side are always square.

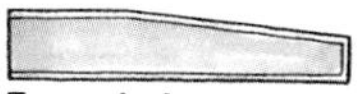

Tapered edge

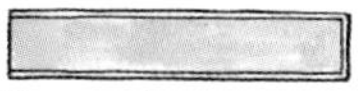

Square edge

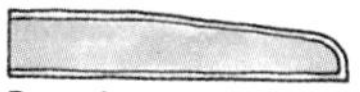

Duo edge

Types of edge
Tapered edges are filled and taped for smooth, seamless jointing. The duo type provides a tapeless option. Square-edged boards can be filled and taped, or plastered over.

STORING AND CUTTING PLASTERBOARD

Plasterboard is fragile, having very little structural strength. Nevertheless, the sheets are quite heavy, so always get someone to help you carry one. Always carry it vertically on edge – there is a serious risk of breaking it if you carry a board face up.

Manufacturers and suppliers of plasterboard store it flat in stacks, but this is usually inconvenient at home and is anyway not necessary for a small number of sheets. Store them on edge instead, leaning them at a slight angle against a wall, their ivory-coloured faces together to protect them.

Stack the sheets carefully to avoid damaging their edges.

Cutting plasterboard
You can cut plasterboard with a saw or with a stiff-blade craft knife.

Support a sheet face-side up on lengths of wood laid across trestles. First mark the cutting line on it with the aid of a straightedge. When sawing, hold the saw at a shallow angle to the surface of the plasterboard. If the offcut is a large one, ask a helper to support it as you approach the end of the cut in order to prevent the board breaking.

When slicing plasterboard with a knife, cut fairly deeply into the material following a straightedge, then snap the board along the cutting line over a length of wood. Cut through the paper facing on the other side to separate the two pieces.

Employ a keyhole saw, a power jigsaw or a craft knife to make openings in plasterboard for switches and other electrical fittings.

Remove any ragged paper after cutting by rubbing down the edges with an abrasive paper.

PLASTERBOARD SPECIFICATIONS

PLASTERBOARD: TYPES AND USAGE	WIDTHS	LENGTHS	THICKNESS	EDGE FINISH
Standard wallboard and plank				
This material is generally used for the dry-lining of walls and ceilings. It is produced in a range of lengths, and though most suppliers stock only a limited selection, other sizes can be ordered. One side is ivory-coloured for direct decoration and the other is grey for plastering.	600mm (2ft) 900mm (3ft) 1.2 (4ft)	1.8m (6ft) to 3.6m (12ft) *Commonly stocked in 2.43m (8ft) and 3.0m (10ft) lengths*	9.5mm (⅜in) 12.5mm (½in) 12.5mm (½in) 15mm (⅝in)	Tapered, duo or square
	Plank 600mm (2ft)	2.35m (7ft 8½in) to 3m (10ft)	19mm (¾in)	Square
Baseboard				
Baseboard is a square-edged plasterboard that is lined with grey paper and is produced as a backing for a plaster finish. It is used mainly for plastered ceilings. It is also available as vapour-check grade (see below).	900mm (3ft)	1.2m (4ft) 1.22m (4ft) 1.37m (4ft 6in)	9.5mm (⅜in)	Square
Lath board				
Lath board is used similarly to baseboard, but its long edges are rounded.	400mm (1ft 4in)	1.2m (4ft) 1.22m (4ft) 1.35m (4ft 5in) 1.37m (4ft 6in)	9.5mm (⅜in) 12.5mm (½in)	Round
Thermal-insulation board				
Thermal-insulation boards are standard sheets of plasterboard with a backing of expanded-polystyrene or urethane laminate. The paper surface may be ivory-coloured for direct decoration or grey for plastering.	1.2m (4ft)	2.4m (7ft 10½in) 2.7m (8ft 10¼in)	25mm (1in)* 30mm (1⅛in) 32mm (1¼in)* 35mm (1⅜in) 40mm (1⅝in)* 45mm (1¾in) 50mm (2in)	Tapered or square
Vapour-check plasterboard				
These boards have a tough metallized polyester-film backing which is vapour-resistant and provides reflective thermal insulation. They are used as an internal lining to prevent warm moist air condensing on or inside structural wall or ceiling materials.	900mm (3ft) 1.2m (4ft)	*Stocked in similar lengths to standard board.*	*Stocked in same thicknesses as standard wallboard.*	Tapered or square

N.B. Metric sizes actual, imperial sizes approximate   *Urethane-backed

PLASTER-BOARDING A WALL

Plasterboard can be nailed directly on to the timber framework of a stud partition or on to wooden battens fixed to a masonry wall. It can also be bonded straight on to solid walls with plaster or an adhesive. The boards can be fitted horizontally if it is more economical to do so, but generally they are placed vertically. All of the edges should be supported. When plasterboarding a ceiling and walls, cover the ceiling first.

Methods of fixing plasterboard

Nailing to a stud partition
Timber-framed partition walls may simply be plain room-dividers or they may include doorways. Start fitting boards from one corner when you are plasterboarding a plain wall; if the wall includes a doorway, work away from it towards the corners of the room.

Starting from a corner
Using a footlifter, try the first board in position. Mark and scribe the edge that meets the adjacent wall if this is necessary, then nail the board into position (see far right), securing it to all the frame members.

Fix the rest of the boards in place, working across the partition. Butt the edges of tapered-edge boards, but leave a gap of 3mm (⅛in) between boards that are going to be coated with a board-finishing plaster.

If necessary, scribe the edge of the last board to fit the end corner before nailing it into place.

Cut a skirting board, mitring the joints at the corners or scribing the ends of the new board to the original. Fit the skirting board.

Starting from a doorway
Using the footlifter, hold a board flush with the door stud and mark the position of the underside of the door head on the edge of the board. Between this mark and the top edge of the board, cut out a 25mm (1in) wide strip. Reposition the board and fix it in place, nailing it to all the frame members (see right).

Fix the rest of the boards in place, working towards the corner. Butt the edges of tapered-edge boards, but leave a 3mm (⅛in) gap between boards that you intend to coat afterwards with a board-finishing plaster.

If necessary, scribe the last board to fit any irregularities in the corner before fixing it in place.

Cover the rest of the wall on the other side of the doorway in a similar way, starting by cutting a 25mm (1in) wide strip from the first board between its top edge and a mark indicating the lower side of the door head.

Cut a plasterboard panel to go above the doorway, butting into the cutouts in the boards on each side of the door. Sand away the ragged edges of paper before fitting the panel.

Clad the other side of the partition with plasterboard in the same way.

When all of the plasterboard is in place, fill and finish the joints. Cut and fit solid-wood door linings and cover the edges with an architrave moulding.

Cut and fit skirting boards, nailing through the plasterboard into alternate studs behind.

NAIL FIXING

Use special galvanized plasterboard nails of lengths appropriate to the thickness of the plasterboard, as shown in the table below.

Space the nails 150mm (6in) apart and place them not less than 9mm (⅜in) from the paper-covered edge and 12mm (½in) from the cut ends. Drive the nails in straight so that their heads sink just below the surface without tearing through the paper lining.

Board thickness	Nail length
9.5mm (⅜in)	32mm (1¼in)
12.5mm (½in)	40mm (1⅝in)
15mm (⅝in)	40mm (1⅝in)
19mm (¾in)	50mm (2in)
25mm (1in)	50mm (2in)
30mm (1⅛in)	65mm (2½in)
32mm (1¼in)	65mm (2½in)
35mm (1⅜in)	65mm (2½in)
40mm (1⅝in)	65mm (2½in)
45mm (1¾in)	75mm (3in)
50mm (2in)	75mm (3in)

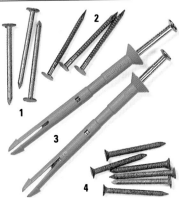

Types of nail used with plasterboard

SEE ALSO

Details for:	
Filling nails	46
Finishing joints	46–47
Skirtings	59
Door casings	61, 64

Fixing to metal studs
Some modern houses may have metal-stud partition walls. If you need to fix into these studs, use special self-tapping drywall screws.

Plasterboard nails
1 Galvanized nails
2 Ring-shank nails
3 Nailable plugs
4 Jagged nails

Distances between stud centres
When providing new supports it is cheaper to use 12.5mm (½in) thick board on studs set 600mm (2ft) apart. Maximum distance between stud centres: for 9.5mm (⅜in) board, 450mm (1ft 6in); for 12.5mm to 50mm (½ to 2in) thick board, 600mm (2ft).

Using a footlifter
Cut the board about 16mm (⅝in) below room height to clear the footlifter, a simple tool that holds the board against the ceiling leaving both hands free for nailing. You can make one from a 75mm (3in) wide block of wood.

Procedure for plasterboarding
Work away from a corner for a plain wall, otherwise work away from a doorway.

SCRIBING
PLASTERBOARD

If the inner edge of the first sheet of plasterboard butts against an uneven wall, or its other edge does not fall on the centre of the stud, the board must be scribed to fit.

Scribing the first board

Try the first board in position (**1**). The illustration shows an uneven wall pushing the plasterboard beyond the stud at the other edge of the sheet of plasterboard.

Reposition the board (**2**) so that its inner edge lies on the centre of the stud and hold it at the required height, using a footlifter. Tack it in place with plasterboard nails driven partway into the intermediate studs.

With a pencil and a batten (cut to the width of the board) trace a line down the face of the wall, making sure you keep the batten level.

Take the board down and use a craft knife or saw to trim the waste away from the scribed edge. Replace the board in the corner and fix it to the studs with plasterboard nails (**3**).

Scribing the last board

Temporarily nail the board to be scribed over the last fixed board (**4**), ensuring that their edges lie flush.

Using a batten and a pencil as above, trace a pencil line down the face of the board, using the batten as a guide and carefully keeping it level.

Remove the marked board, cut along the scribed line, then nail the board to the studs (**5**).

Fill and tape the joints or apply finish plaster as required.

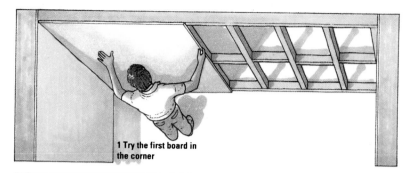

1 Try the first board in the corner

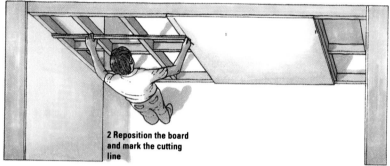

2 Reposition the board and mark the cutting line

3 Cut the board to size and nail in place

4 Temporarily nail the last board and scribe it to fit

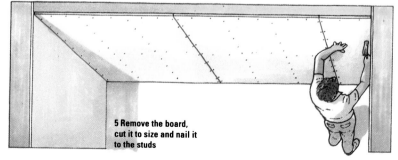

5 Remove the board, cut it to size and nail it to the studs

Plasterboard cannot be nailed directly to masonry walls, so battens of sawn timber known as furring strips are used to provide a good fixing for the nails and to counter any unevenness of the wall surface. These should be treated with a wood preserver. You can cover old plaster if it is sound, but if not strip it back to the brickwork. If damp has damaged the original plaster, it must be treated and, if possible, the area should be allowed to dry out before lining. Fix any plumbing pipe runs, electrical conduit or cable to the wall before the battens are fixed to conceal them.

Marking out

Use a straightedge to mark the position of the battens on the wall with vertical chalk lines. The lines should be placed at 400mm (1ft 4in), 450mm (1ft 6in) or 600mm (2ft) centres according to the width and thickness of the plasterboard being used. Bear in mind that sheets of plasterboard must meet on the centre lines of the battens. Work away from any door or window opening and allow for the thickness of the battens and plasterboard at the reveals.

Fixing the battens

Cut the required number of furring battens from 50 x 32mm (2 x 1¼in) sawn softwood. The vertical battens should be cut 155mm (6¼in) less than the height of the wall. Horizontal battens should be made to run along the tops and bottoms of the vertical ones and any short vertical infill battens above and below openings (see below).

Nail the vertical furring battens on first, setting their bottom ends 100mm (4in) above the floor. Fix them with masonry nails or cut nails, with the face of each batten level with the guideline (see right), and check with a straightedge and spirit level that they are also flat and plumb, packing them out as necessary.

Now nail the horizontal battens across the tops and bottoms of the vertical members, inserting packing to bring them all to the same level.

Fixing the plasterboard

To fix plasterboard to furring battens, follow the procedure described for nailing to a stud partition. However, the boards at the sides of windows and doors need not be notched to receive panels above or below the openings. The procedure for filling and finishing joints between the boards is identical. Cut the skirting board to length and nail it through the plasterboard to the bottom horizontal furring batten. If it is a high moulded skirting of the type used in period houses, it can be nailed to the vertical battens.

LEVELLING THE FURRING BATTENS

Masonry walls are often uneven and, if the lining is to finish straight and flat, this must be taken into account. To check if the wall is flat, hold a long straightedge horizontally against it at different levels. If it is uneven, mark the vertical chalk line already drawn on the wall which is the closest to the point where the wall bulges most (1).

Hold a straight furring batten vertically on the marked chalk line keeping it plumb with a straightedge and spirit level, then mark the floor (2) where the edge of the batten falls. Draw a straight guideline across the floor (3), passing through this mark and meeting the walls on each end at right angles. Align all furring battens with this line.

1 Check the wall

2 Mark the high point

3 Draw line on floor

Aligning the battens
Use a straightedge to align the battens

Attaching furring battens to a wall
1 Mark batten positions.
2 Fix vertical battens.
3 Attach horizontal battens.
4 Fix short pieces over doors and windows and offset the short vertical ones.
5 Nail boards in place, working away from a door or window.

BONDING TO
A SOLID WALL

As an alternative to using batten fixing for dry-lining a solid wall, tapered-edge plasterboard can be bonded directly to the wall with dabs of plaster or adhesive. Rectangular pads about 100 x 50mm (4 x 2in) cut from remnants of plasterboard are used for levelling the wall. The pads are bonded to the wall in lines as substitutes for battens and allowed to set. Dabs of plaster are then applied between the pads and the plasterboard is temporarily nailed to the pads while the plaster sets.

Boards 900mm (3ft) wide are normally used for this technique. The wall must be prepared in the usual way.

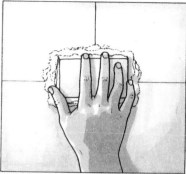
1 Bond first pad on marked intersection

Fixing the pads

Set out vertical chalk lines on the wall 450mm (1ft 6in) apart, working from one corner or from an opening (see below). Draw a horizontal line 225mm (9in) from the ceiling, one 100mm (4in) from the floor and another centred between them. If the wall is more than 2.4m (8ft) high, divide the space between the top and bottom equally with two lines. The pads are placed where the horizontal and vertical lines intersect.

Using a spirit level and a straightedge that is almost the full height of the wall, check at each vertical line, noting high spots at the intersections of the lines.

Bond a pad on the most prominent intersection point (**1**), using a bonding-coat plaster or a proprietary tile adhesive, and press it in place. This pad forms the datum point from which the rest of the pads are levelled.

Bond and plumb the other pads on the same vertical line, then complete a second vertical row, two lines from the first. Check these pads for level vertically then diagonally with the first row. Work across the wall in this way, then fix the remaining pads on the other intersections. Allow two hours for the adhesive to set.

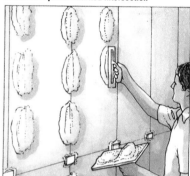
2 Apply thick dabs of plaster between the pads

Fixing the plasterboard

Apply thick dabs of bonding plaster to the wall with a trowel (**2**) over an area for one board at a time. Space the dabs 75mm (3in) apart vertically. Do not let the plaster overlap the area of the next board. Using the straightedge to press it evenly and a footlifter to position it, press the board firmly against the pads so that the plaster spreads out behind it.

Check the alignment, then fix the board with plasterboard nails driven into the pads round the edge. Do not drive the nails in fully. Fix the next board in the same way, butting it to the first, and work on across the wall, scribing the last board into the internal angle. When the plaster has set, remove the nails with pincers or a claw hammer, protecting the plasterboard surface (**3**).

Work round angles and openings (see opposite) and, when all surfaces are covered, fill and finish the joints.

3 Pull out the nails when the plaster has set

Bonding plasterboard to a wall
1 Mark pad positions.
2 Stick the pads over the intersections.
3 Apply dabs of plaster to the wall.
4 Place plasterboard and nail temporarily. Remove nails when plaster has set.

WINDOW OPENINGS

Cut plasterboard linings to fit the soffit and window reveals, and attach them before you apply the boards that line the wall. Align the front edges of the window linings with the faces of the battens or allow for dabs of plaster.

Apply evenly spaced dabs of plaster adhesive to the back of the soffit lining, press it into place (1) and prop it there while the adhesive sets. If the lining bridges a wide span, support it with a wooden board before you prop it. Fit the reveal linings in the same way (2).

Working away from the window, fix the wall linings so that the paper-covered edge of the board laps the cut edge of the reveal lining.

The panels for above and below the window are cut and fitted last. Sand off rough edges of paper and leave a 3mm (⅛in) gap between boards for filling.

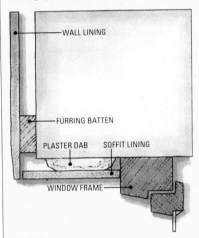

1 Soffit lining
Fix a soffit lining with dabs of plaster adhesive and prop in place until set.

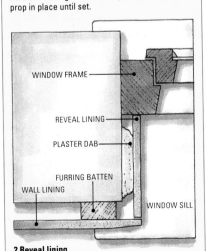

2 Reveal lining
Like the soffit lining, cut and fix the reveal so the wall lining overlaps its cut edge.

Internal angle

Fix wooden furring battens or plasterboard pads close to the corner. Whenever possible, place the cut edges of the plasterboard lining into an internal corner.

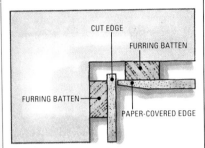

Internal corner
Set cut edges into the angle.

External angle

Attach furring battens or plasterboard pads as close to the corner as possible. Use screws and wall plugs to fix the battens so as to prevent the corner breaking away. At least one board should have a paper-covered edge, which should lap the other.

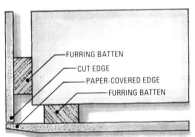

External corner
A paper-covered edge should lap the outer edge.

Door openings

Line the reveals and soffits of doorways in exterior walls as described for window openings (see far left).
In the case of interior door openings, screw-fix timber furring battens or bond plasterboard pads level with the edge of the wall, then nail the plasterboard linings in place.

Fit a new door lining (or modify the old one) and cover the joint with an architrave moulding.

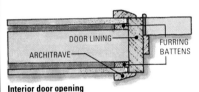

Interior door opening
Fit a new lining or widen the old one and cover the joint between the lining and plasterboard with an architrave moulding.

Electrical fittings

Depending on the type of fitting, chase the wall or pack out the mounting box for an electrical switch or socket outlet so that it finishes flush with the face of the plasterboard lining. Screw-fix short lengths of furring batten at each side of the box or use dabs of adhesive.

Cut the opening for the box before fixing the board. If you find it difficult to mark the opening accurately by transferring measurements, remove the fitting from its mounting box and take an impression by placing the board in position and pressing it against the box.

Fix the plasterboard panel in place and replace the electrical fitting.

Electrical fittings
Turn off the power before you dismantle electrical fittings. Chase the wall or pack out the mounting box to set it flush with the plasterboard.

Lining door and window openings
1 Fit soffit lining.
2 Fit reveal lining.
3 Fit boards, working away from window.
4 Fit panels above and below window.
5 Fit boarding, working away from doorway.
6 Cut and fit panel above doorway.
7 Cut openings for electrical fittings.

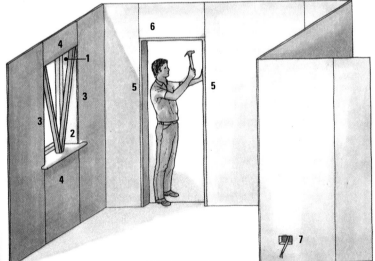

FINISHING
PLASTERBOARD

All joints between boards and indentations left by nailing must be filled and smoothed before the ivory-coloured surface of plasterboard is ready for decorating. You will need jointing tape, filler and a special plaster-based 'finish' that leaves a smooth feathered joint.

Tools and materials

The filler and finish are prepared for use by being mixed with water. The paper jointing tape is 53mm (2⅛in) wide with feathered edges, and is creased along its centre. It is used for reinforcing flat joints and internal angles. A special paper jointing tape is available for covering and reinforcing external angles. This tape has thin metal strips on each side of its central crease which strengthen the corners.

Professional plasterers use purpose-made tools for finishing joints, but you can use medium and wide filling knives, a plasterer's trowel and a close-textured plastic sponge.

Covering nails

Fill the indentations that have been left by nailing, using a filling knife to apply then smooth the filler. When the filler has set, apply a thin coating of joint finish and feather it off at the edges with a damp sponge.

Filling tapered-edge joints

Mix joint filler to a creamy consistency and apply a continuous band of it about 60mm (2½in) wide down the length of each joint.

Press the paper tape into the filler, using a medium-size filling knife to bed it in well and exclude air bubbles (1). Follow this with another layer of filler applied over the tape to level the surface, this time using the wide filling knife. When the filler has stiffened slightly, smooth its edges with the damp sponge, then let it set completely before filling any remaining small hollows.

When all the filler has set, coat it with a thin layer of joint finish. Mix the finish thoroughly to the consistency of thick cream and apply it in a broad band down the joint, using a wide filler knife or trowel (2). Before it sets, feather its edges with a dampened sponge.

After the joint finish has set, apply another thin but wider band over the first application, again feathering the edges with the sponge, working with a circular motion (3).

CUT EDGES

When a square-cut edge of plasterboard butts against a tapered-edge board, fill the joint flush before you apply the jointing tape (1).

Where two cut edges meet (2), press filler into the 3mm (⅛in) gap to finish flush. When the filler has set, apply a thin band of joint finish to it and press the paper tape tight against the board. Cover this with a wide but thin coat of finish and feather the edges. Finish off as before.

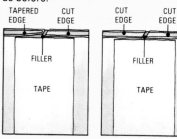

1 Tapered-edge joint   2 Square-edged joint

GLASS-FIBRE TAPE

A self-adhesive glass-fibre mesh tape can be used instead of traditional paper tape for jointing new plasterboard or for making patch repairs. The 50mm (2in) wide tape is a strong binder and does not need prior application of filler to bond it in place. The tape is applied first, then joint filler is pressed through the mesh.

Applying the tape
Ensure that the jointing edges of the plasterboard are dust-free. If the edges of boards have been cut, burnish them with the handle of your filling knife to remove all traces of rough paper.

Starting at the top, centre the tape over the joint, then unroll it and press it in place as you work down the wall. Cut it off to length at the bottom. Butt the ends rather than overlap them if you have to make a join in the tape.

Mix the filler and press it through the tape into the joint with a filling knife, then level off the surface so that the mesh of the tape is visible. Allow the filler to set.

Complete the joint with plaster-based joint finish, as with paper tape.

Applying filler
Press the filler through the tape with a flexible filling knife.

1 Press tape into filler

2 Apply finish in a wide band

3 Feather edge with a sponge

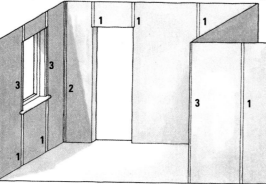

Filling the joints
1 Use the tape flat for flush jointing.
2 Fold the tape for internal corners.
3 Use metal-reinforced tape or metal beading on external corners.

46

FINISHING
PLASTERBOARD

Internal corners

The internal corners of dry-lined walls are finished by a method similar to that used for flat joints. Any gaps are first filled flush with filler and if necessary a band of PVA bonding agent is applied to the original ceiling or wall plaster to reduce its suction.

Cut the paper tape to length and fold it down its centre. Brush a thin band of finish on to each side of the corner and press the tape into it while it is still wet. Use a square-section length of wood to press down both sides at once to remove air bubbles (1).

With a filling knife, apply a 75mm (3in) wide band of finish to both sides of the corner immediately and feather the edges with a damp sponge (2). When the finish has set, apply a second, wider coat and feather the edges again.

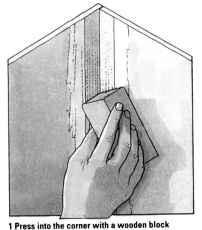

1 Press into the corner with a wooden block

2 Apply a wide band of finish and feather edge

External corners

When finishing an external-corner joint, use metal-reinforced corner tape. Cut it to length, fold it down its centre, then apply a 50mm (2in) wide band of filler down both sides of the corner and press the tape onto it, using a wide filling knife to keep the corner straight. Press the tape down well so that the metal strips are bedded firmly against the face of the plasterboard. If you have used tapered-edge board, however, square up the corner with filler before you apply the tape (1). Apply two coats of joint finish, feathering the edges as described for internal corners.

Protect a vulnerable corner with a length of metal angle bead. Apply a coating of filler to each side of the corner, then bed the angle bead in it, smoothing the filler flush with a knife before leaving it to set (2).

Apply a second coat of filler to both sides in a wide band and feather it off with a damp sponge.

When the filler has set, apply two coats of finish, feathering off as before.

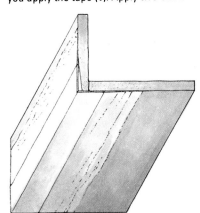

1 Fill out a tapered-edge board, then bed tape

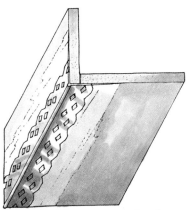

2 Embed metal bead in filler and feather edge

PREPARING FOR DECORATION

Finishing with plaster

As an alternative to direct decoration of the ivory-coloured side of plasterboard, apply a thin coat of board-finish plaster to the grey face.

Applying a thin finishing coat is not an easy technique to master, but with some practice you may be able to tackle the walls. However, it pays to leave the plastering of ceilings to a professional, though you can still prepare the plasterboard (see below) and have it ready for the tradesman. If you decide to attempt the plastering yourself, study the section on plastering thoroughly before you begin.

Preparing the background

First fill flush with the surface all joints and gaps between boards and at the corners. Reinforce them with strips of jute scrim pressed into a thin band of plaster. Rolls of jute scrim, 90mm (3½in) wide, are available from the majority of builders' merchants.

Let the plaster set, but not dry out thoroughly, before applying a coat of finishing plaster.

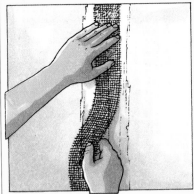

Reinforce joints with scrim before plastering

Decorating directly

Before the ivory-coloured side of plasterboard can be decorated it must be given a uniform surface by the application of a sealer. Brush or sponge-apply a thin coating of joint finish mixed to a thin consistency. If you paint it on, follow up with the sponge, working with a light circular motion over the entire surface. Alternatively, use a proprietary ready-mixed top coat which can be applied with a brush or roller and is suitable for all decorative treatments. Two coats will also provide a vapour barrier.

PLASTER- BOARDING A CEILING

Plasterboard is usually employed to make new ceilings, but it can also be used to replace an old lath-and-plaster ceiling which has deteriorated beyond repair.

Fixing the plasterboard in place and finishing its surface ready for decorating can be tackled by a competent amateur, but applying wet-plaster to a boarded ceiling should be left to a skilled tradesman – it is strenuous work and extremely difficult to perfect.

Preparing an old ceiling

Start by stripping away all the old and damaged plaster and laths, and pull out all the nails.

This is a messy job, so wear protective clothing, a pair of goggles and a face mask while working. It is also a good idea to seal the gaps round doors in the room to prevent dust escaping into the rest of the house. You will need to dispose of a surprising amount of waste material, so have a number of strong plastic sacks available to make it easier to handle, and hire a skip to have it removed.

If necessary, trim back the top of the wall plaster so that the edge of the ceiling plasterboard can be tucked in.

Inspect and treat the exposed joists for any signs of woodworm or rot.

Working single-handedly

1 Support the boards with simple T-shaped props called dead-men.

2 Nail a batten to the wall to give temporary support to the long edge of the board.

3 Nail a temporary support batten to the ceiling joists when butting boards.

Boarding a ceiling
1 Cut and fit perimeter noggings against the wall.
2 Nail intermediate noggings between the joists to suit the width of the boarding.
3 Fix the first board in one corner. Start nailing from the centre of the board.
4 Butt the side joints for direct decoration or leave a 3mm (⅛in) gap if plastering over.
5 Stagger the end joints, leaving a 3mm (⅛in) gap in all cases.

FITTING NEW BOARDING

Measure the area of ceiling and select the most economical size of boards to cover it.

The boards should be fitted with their long paper-covered edges running at right angles to the joists. The butt joints between the ends of the boards should be staggered on each row and supported by a joist in every case.

Skew-nail perimeter noggings between the joists against the walls, and fit intermediate ones in lines across the ceiling to support the long edges of the boards. It is not always necessary to fit intermediate noggings if the boards are going to be plastered, but they will ensure a sound ceiling. The intermediate noggings should be at least 50mm (2in) thick and should be fitted so that the edges of the boards will fall along their centre lines.

If necessary, trim the length of the boards to ensure that their ends fall on the centre lines of the joists.

Start fixing the boards, working from one corner of the room. Plasterboard is a relatively heavy material and it normally takes two people to support a large and awkward sheet while it is being fixed (see below). However, if you have to work on your own, use support battens and props, called 'dead-men', to hold the boards in place while you are nailing them (see far left).

Make a pair of props that are slightly longer than the overall height of the room (**1**) from 50 x 50mm (2 x 2in) softwood. Nail a cross piece and braces to one end of each prop. You will need to nail a 50 x 25mm (2 x 1in) temporary batten close to the top of the wall to support the long edges of the first row of boards (**2**). Support the next row with a batten that overlaps the edges of the first boards and is nailed to the joists (**3**). Fit packing under the batten to provide the necessary clearance for the new boards.

Use galvanized plasterboard nails to fix each board, working from the middle outwards and nailing at 150mm (6in) centres. This prevents the boards from sagging in the middle, which is likely to happen if their edges are nailed first.

If the boards are to be plastered, leave 3mm (⅛in) gaps between the cut ends and the paper-covered edges. For direct decoration, however, butt the paper-covered edges, but leave 3mm (⅛in) gaps at the ends of each board.

Finish the joints, using the method described for plasterboard walls.

SEE ALSO

Coving and cornices

A plaster cornice or a simple coving are used to finish the edges of a ceiling where it meets the walls. Ready-made gypsum coving is widely available, generally in a fairly limited range of profile sizes and in various lengths. However, you can buy any number of period-style fibrous-plaster cornices, many of which are exact copies of Georgian and Victorian originals.

Templates are sometimes provided by the makers which are intended to be used as guides when you are cutting the internal and external mitre joints.

Fitting a cornice or coving

This sequence describes how to make a coved ceiling, but you can use the same method to fit a cornice.

Start by marking parallel lines along the wall and ceiling, setting them off from the angle at the distance specified in the manufacturer's instructions, then scratch the plastered surfaces within the lines in order to provide a good key for the adhesive (1).

Measure the wall and cut the coving to fit, using the template to saw the mitre (see right). Remember that when you are cutting mitres for outside corners, the coving must be longer than the wall, and must extend up to the line of the return angle drawn on the ceiling. Cut the coving with a fine-toothed saw, sawing from the face side.

Prepare the special adhesive by mixing the powder with clean water and stirring it to a creamy consistency. The adhesive should remain usable for about 30 minutes, but it is best to aim at making just enough for one length of coving at a time. Use a filling knife to apply the adhesive liberally to the back faces of the coving which will be in contact with the wall and ceiling.

Dry, bare plaster must be dampened just before the coving is put in place. Press it into the angle and level it with the guidelines (2). If a piece of coving is more than about 2m (6ft 6in) long, two people should fit it. Should it tend to sag when in place, support it with a couple of nails driven temporarily into the wall under its bottom edge and remove them when the adhesive has set.

Scrape away any beads of surplus adhesive before it sets and use it to fill the mitre joints as the work progresses. Use your finger to apply the adhesive to internal mitres if you find it easier, but finish off all joints with a filling knife to leave a sharp corner (3).

Wipe along the edges of the coving with a damp brush or sponge to remove any traces of adhesive. When it dries, prime the coving for painting.

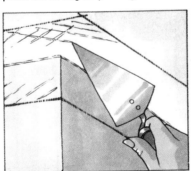
Fitted coving at external and internal corner

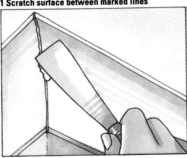
2 Press the coving into angle, level with the lines

1 Scratch surface between marked lines

3 Finish off with a filling knife

CUTTING THE MITRES

Using a template

Some makers of plaster coving and cornice supply a cardboard template with their product, which enables you to cut mitred corners more easily.

Mark the coving or cornice to length on one edge, bearing in mind whether you are mitring for an external corner or an internal one. Trim and fold the template and place it over the coving in line with the measured mark, then press it down so that it moulds itself to the curve of the material. Use the appropriate edge of the template – for an external or an internal mitre – and, with a soft pencil, draw the cutting line along it on the face and edges of the coving, tracing the template's edge.

Cut the mitre with a fine-toothed saw, following the marked angle.

Using a jig

If you use plaster coving or cornice right through the house, it is worth making a mitre block as a jig to help you cut the joints accurately.

Cut a baseboard from 18mm (¾in) plywood or chipboard about 200mm (8in) wide and 450mm (1ft 6in) long. Cut a piece of 100 x 50mm (4 x 2in) planed softwood to the same length for a fence.

Glue the fence to the baseboard flush with one long edge. When the adhesive has set, mark out and make three saw cuts, one at right angles to the face of the fence and two at 45 degrees in opposite directions. Nail a stop batten to the baseboard at a distance from the fence which will allow the coving to fit snugly between them for cutting.

The baseboard of the mitre block represents the ceiling and the fence represents the wall. Lay the coving in the jig with the end to be cut in the right direction for either an external or an internal mitre (see right).

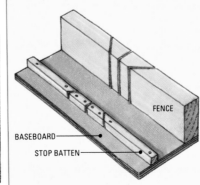
FENCE

BASEBOARD

STOP BATTEN

Make a mitre block for cutting joints accurately

Cornice profile

Coving profile

External mitre

1 Left-hand piece

2 Right-hand piece

Internal mitre

1 Left-hand piece

2 Right-hand piece

49

FLOORS:
SUSPENDED
FLOORS

Floor construction in the majority of buildings is based on timber beams known as joists. These are rectangular in section, placed on edge for maximum strength, usually about 400mm (1ft 4in) apart, and supported at the ends by the walls.

Such 'suspended floors' contrast with concrete 'solid floors' – supported over their whole area by the ground – which are usually to be found in basements and commonly at ground level in modern houses.

Traditional suspended floors are usually boarded with tongue-and-groove or plain-edged planks, though in modern houses flooring-grade chipboard is used on both types of floor.

Ground floors

The joists of a suspended ground floor are usually made from 100 x 50mm (4 x 2in) sawn softwood. Their ends and centre portions are nailed to lengths of 100 x 75mm (4 x 3in) softwood called wall plates that distribute the load from the joists to the walls, which support the weight of the floor.

In older houses, various methods were employed for supporting the wall plates. At one time it was common for the ends of the joists to be slotted into the walls and set on wall plates that were built into the brickwork.

Alternatively, the brickwork was formed so as to provide ledges – known as offsets – to support the wall plates. However, when the damp-proof courses laid beneath the wall plates broke down, the wood was affected by penetrating and rising damp in the brickwork. As a result, such floor timbers frequently suffer from decay.

The relatively lightweight joists tend to sag in the middle and are therefore usually supported by additional wall plates set on three or four courses of honeycombed brickwork known as sleeper walls. The spaces left in the brickwork allow air to circulate under the floor. Sleeper walls are usually spaced at intervals of about 2m (6ft), and are sometimes used to support the ends of the joists.

Beneath a fireplace in a room with a suspended floor will be found a solid brick wall, built to the same height as the sleeper walls. It retains and supports the concrete hearth. This fender wall carries a wall plate along its top edge to support the ends of the floor joists that run up to it.

UPPER FLOORS

The first-floor joists and those of other upper floors can be supported only at their ends, so they are usually laid in the direction of the shortest span. Also, as they can have no intermediate support, such joists are made deeper to give them greater rigidity. These 'bridging joists' are usually 50mm (2in) thick, but their depth will be determined by the distance they must span. The joists supporting the floor of an average-size upper room would be about 225mm (9in) deep.

Where floor joists cannot run right through – as around a fireplace or at a stairway opening – a thicker joist is used to bear the extra load of the short joists. This load is transferred to the thicker joist by crosspieces jointed at right angles (see left). The thicker joist is known as a 'trimming joist', the short ones parallel to it are 'trimmed joists' and the crosspieces joining them together are known as 'trimmers'.

In older properties the upstairs joists may be supported on wall plates which are built into solid walls; the problems of damp and decay are less critical here. With modern cavity-wall construction the ends of the joists may also be built in, but in this case they rest directly on the inner skin of blockwork. The joist-ends should not project into the cavity itself, and they must be treated with a preserver to guard against the risk of timber decay.

Components of the first floor
1 Joists
2 Trimming joist
3 Trimmed joist
4 Trimmer
5 Herringbone strutting

Components of the ground floor
6 Oversite concrete
7 Sleeper walls
8 Wall plate
9 Fender wall
10 Floor joists

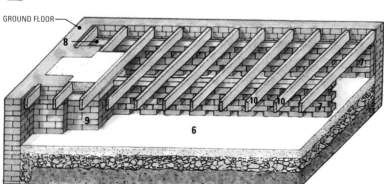

FIRST FLOOR

GROUND FLOOR

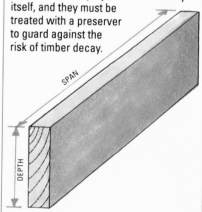

SPAN

DEPTH

To estimate the size of timber for a floor joist use the following rule of thumb as a guide.

Depth in units of 25mm (1in) =

$$\frac{\text{Span of joist in units of 300mm (1ft)}}{2} + 2$$

Examples:
Metric.
Joists span 3m divided by 300mm = 10 units

$$\frac{10 \text{ units}}{2} + 2 = 5 + 2 = 7 \text{ units} \times 25mm = 175mm$$

Imperial.

$$\frac{\text{Joist span 10ft}}{2} + 2 = 5 + 2 = 7 \text{inches}$$

BRACING FLOORS

For extra stiffness the joists of an upper floor are braced with 'solid strutting' – solid sections of timber nailed between them **(1)** – or with diagonal wooden braces called 'herringbone strutting' **(2)**.

The traditional herringbone strutting, of 50 x 25mm (2 x 1in) softwood, is preferable because it can compensate for timber shrinkage. Folded wedges or packing blocks are placed in line with the strutting between the outer joists and the walls to keep the joints tight.

Modern herringbone strutting is carried out with ready-made metal units **(3)** which are usually equipped with a drilled flange at each end for nailing to joists set at 400, 450 or 600mm (1ft 4in, 1ft 6in or 2ft) centres.

1 Solid strutting

2 Herringbone strutting

3 Ready-made metal herringbone strutting

A solid ground floor is essentially a concrete slab laid on a sub-stratum of coarse rubble, or hardcore. To lay such a floor the topsoil is first removed and the hardcore then laid to consolidate the ground and level up the site. The rough surface of the hardcore is filled (blinded) with a thin layer of sand which is rolled flat. This sand layer prevents the cement draining out of the concrete and into the hardcore, which would cause the concrete to be weakened.

The concrete slab is usually about 100 to 150mm (4 to 6in) thick and is either laid over or covered by a continuous layer of moisture-resistant material, the damp-proof membrane, or DPM. This membrane may be a thick sheet of polyethylene or the more traditional liquid coating of asphalt or bituminous material. However it is laid,

the DPM must be joined to the damp-proof course (DPC) set in the walls.

A concrete raft foundation can either form a solid floor on which the walls are built, or, where strip or trench foundations are used, the slab can be laid over the ground contained within the brickwork walls.

The floor must first be covered with a smooth screed of sand and cement before it can be overlaid with a floorcovering. When the DPM is below the concrete slab the screed can be 44mm (1¾in) thick, but when a membrane is laid over the slab the screed should be at least 63mm (2½in) in thickness.

A suspended solid floor is a recent type that uses precast concrete beams set on sleeper walls at DPC level and infilled with concrete blocks.

SOLID GROUND
FLOORS

SEE ALSO
Details for:
Metal fittings 52
Solid floors 53

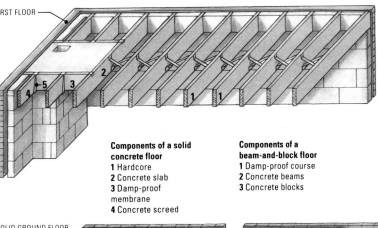

FIRST FLOOR

Components of the first floor
1 Joists
2 Trimming joist
3 Trimmer
4 Trimmed joist
5 Metal hangers

Suspended floor
The construction of a modern suspended first floor is similar to the traditional method, but the ends of the joists are supported by the inner blocks of the cavity wall or by metal hangers. Metal fittings such as straps and framing anchors may also be used to join the timbers to each other or to the walls.

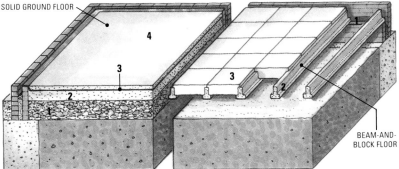

Components of a solid concrete floor
1 Hardcore
2 Concrete slab
3 Damp-proof membrane
4 Concrete screed

Components of a beam-and-block floor
1 Damp-proof course
2 Concrete beams
3 Concrete blocks

SOLID GROUND FLOOR

BEAM-AND-BLOCK FLOOR

Solid floors
A solid floor is often used in preference to a suspended wooden floor as it can be cheaper to construct. A concrete floor can be laid after the foundations and first courses of brickwork are built above ground level, or can be built up using a beam-and-block system, or be an integral part of a reinforced-concrete foundation, forming a raft (see left).

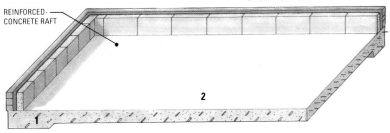

Components of a concrete raft
1 Integral foundation
2 Reinforced-concrete slab

REINFORCED-CONCRETE RAFT

51

METAL FITTINGS FOR FLOORS

Floor construction is one of the many areas in which modern builders have been able to substitute the use of factory-made fittings for traditional methods of construction.

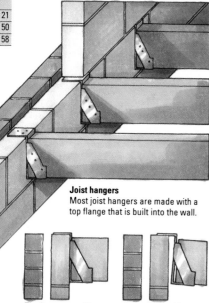

Joist hangers
Most joist hangers are made with a top flange that is built into the wall.

The hanger must be a close fit to the wall

A poorly fitted hanger will distort

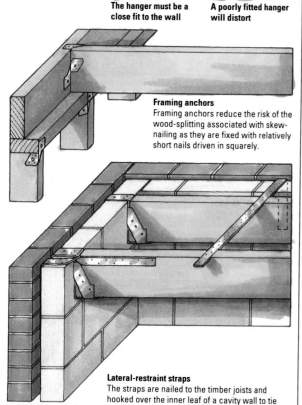

Framing anchors
Framing anchors reduce the risk of the wood-splitting associated with skew-nailing as they are fixed with relatively short nails driven in squarely.

Lateral-restraint straps
The straps are nailed to the timber joists and hooked over the inner leaf of a cavity wall to tie the floor and walls together. They are set at right angles to, or parallel with, the line of the joists.

52

Joist hangers

Galvanized-steel joist hangers are widely used in the construction of upper timber floors. These are brackets which are fastened to masonry walls to support the ends of the joists. There are various versions for securing joists to solid or cavity walls, and special brackets form a similar function when constructing timber-to-timber joints.

The use of metal joist hangers allows brickwork or blockwork to be completely built up before joists are fitted. It also saves having to cut blocks or bricks in order to infill between the ends of joists that are built into the inner leaf of a wall.

The hangers should be fitted properly, with the top flange sitting squarely on the bricks or blocks, and the rear face of the bracket fitting closely against the face of the masonry.

The ends of the joists are fixed into hangers with 32mm (1¼in) sherardized twisted nails or plasterboard nails, one or two being driven through the holes in the side gussets.

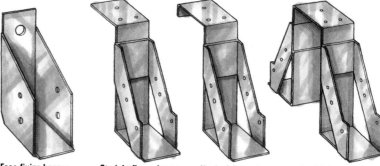

Face-fixing hanger   **Straight-flange hanger**   **Hooked-flange hanger**   **Double hanger**

Framing anchors

Framing anchors are steel brackets used to make butt joints between flooring timbers. They are employed by builders to fix trimmed joists to save them having to cut complicated time-consuming joints.

Framing anchors are made left-handed and right-handed

Lateral-restraint straps

While the walls carry the weight of the floor, the floors contribute lateral stiffness to the walls.

In areas where the force of the wind can threaten the stability of modern lightweight walls, lateral-restraint straps are used to provide ties between the walls and the floor. They are simply rigid strips of galvanized steel that are perforated for nail fixing and bent in various ways to suit the direction of the floor joists.

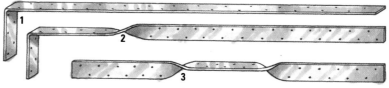

Lateral-restraint straps
1 For tying joists parallel to an external wall.
2 For tying joists at right angles to an external wall.
3 For tying joists on either side of an internal wall.

Most floorcoverings, including woodblock flooring, can be bonded directly to a dry, smooth, screeded floor, but floorboards cannot be directly bonded and so must be fixed by other means.

The boards are nailed down to 50 x 50mm (2 x 2in) softwood battens, or bearers. These battens are embedded in the concrete while it is wet or are fixed to metal clips which are already implanted in the concrete. In either case the timber must be treated with a wood preserver. A damp-proof membrane (DPM) must be incorporated, usually in the form of a continuous coat of bituminous material sandwiched within the slab.

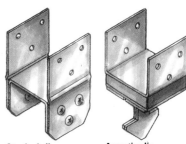

Standard clip   **Acoustic clip**

SEE ALSO
Details for:
Flooring   54

The clip method

This means of fixing requires the slab to be level and relatively smooth. The flanges of the clips are pressed into the surface of the concrete before it sets, while a marked guide batten is used to space the clips and align them in rows. The rows are normally set 400mm (1ft 4in) apart to centres, starting 50mm (2in) from one wall. When the concrete is completely dry the 'ears' of the clips are raised from their folded position with a claw hammer. The battens, having been cut to length and their ends treated with a preserver, are nailed in place through the holes in the clips. The boards are nailed to the battens.

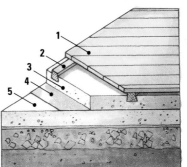

1 Clip method
Composition of floor
1 Floorboards
2 Clipped battens
3 Concrete screed
4 DPM
5 Concrete slab

Embedded battens

These are splayed in section so as to key into the concrete slab. Again, the slab is built up in two layers with the DPM sandwiched between them. Before the top layer or screed is laid, the treated battens are positioned at 400mm (1ft 4in) centres and levelled on dabs of concrete. Strips of wood are nailed across them temporarily to hold them in position. When the dabs of concrete are set and the battens firmly held, the wood strips are removed and the top layer of concrete is poured and compacted. It is levelled with a rule that is notched to fit over the battens. As the rule is drawn along the battens, it finishes the concrete 12mm (½in) below their top edges. When the concrete layer is fully dry the boards are nailed on the battens in the conventional way.

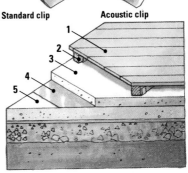

2 Embedded battens
Composition of floor
1 Floorboards
2 Embedded battens
3 Concrete screed
4 DPM
5 Concrete slab

Chipboard floating floor

Flooring-grade chipboard is a relatively recent innovation as a material for boarding over a solid floor. It is quicker and cheaper to lay than a floor made of boards. Chipboard flooring is also more stable and it can be laid without being fixed to the concrete slab.

This technique produces a floor of the type known as a 'floating floor'. The simplest floor of this kind is laid with 18mm (¾in) tongue-and-groove chipboard, either the standard grade or the moisture-resistant type.

First a sheet of insulating material such as rigid polystyrene or fibreboard is laid on the concrete slab; then a vapour barrier of polyethylene sheet is laid above the polystyrene. The vapour barrier must be a continuous sheet, with its edges turned up and trapped behind the skirting boards. The chipboard, glued edge to edge, is then laid on the vapour barrier.

The chipboard flooring is held in place by its own weight and by the skirting boards, which are nailed to the walls round its edges. The skirting boards also cover a 9mm (⅜in) gap between the chipboard and the walls, allowing for expansion across the floor.

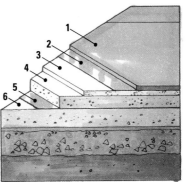

3 Chipboard floating floor
1 Chipboard flooring
2 Vapour barrier
3 Polystyrene insulation
4 Concrete screed
5 DPM
6 Concrete Slab

Battened floating floor

Battens can be incorporated in a floating floor. Lengths of 50 x 50mm (2 x 2in) softwood, treated with a preserver, are spaced at 400mm (1ft 4in) intervals for 18mm (¾in) chipboard; for heavy-gauge 22mm (⅞in) material they are spaced 600mm (2ft) apart. A quilt-type sheet of insulating material is laid on the concrete slab, then covered with a polyethylene vapour barrier. The battens are positioned on the insulation, held together temporarily with strips of wood nailed across them. Tongue-and-groove chipboard is laid at right angles to the battens and glued at the edges before it is nailed down.

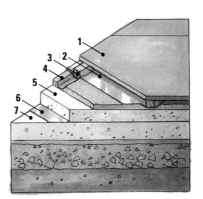

4 Battened floating floor
1 Chipboard flooring
2 Vapour barrier
3 Battens
4 Insulation
5 Concrete screed
6 DPM
7 Concrete slab

FLOORING

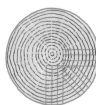

1 Quarter-sawn boards
Shrinkage does not
distort these boards

**2 Tangentially
sawn boards**
Shrinkage can
cause these
boards to 'cup'

Types of flooring
1 Square-edged
softwood board
2 T & G softwood board
3 Square-edged
chipboard
4 T & G chipboard
5 Square-edged
plywood
6 T & G plywood
7 Square-edged MDF

Flooring is the general term used to describe the boarding which is laid over the floor's structural elements – the timber floor joists or the concrete slab. This boarding consists of hardwood or softwood planks, or man-made boards.

Floorboards

Floorboards are usually made from softwoods and sold planed all round (PAR) with square or tongue-and-groove edges. Standard sizes are specified as 125 x 25mm (5 x 1in) or 150 x 25mm (6 x 1in) nominal.

However, boards as narrow as 75mm (3in) and others as wide as 280mm (11in) may be found in some houses. The narrow boards produce superior floors because they make any movement due to shrinkage less noticeable. Installation costs are high, and consequently they tend to be used in more expensive houses only. Hardwoods, such as oak or maple, are also used for high-grade flooring but are even more costly.

The best floorboards are quarter sawn **(1)** from the log, a method that diminishes distortion due to shrinkage. However, since this method is wasteful of timber, boards are more often cut tangentially **(2)** for reasons of economy. Boards cut in this way tend to bow, or 'cup', across their width and they should be fixed with the concave side facing upwards, as there is a tendency for the grain of the other side to splinter. The cut of a board – tangential or quarter cut – can be checked by looking at the annual-growth rings on the end grain.

The joint on tongue-and-groove boards is not at the centre of their edges but closer to one face, and these boards should be laid with the offset joint nearer to the joist. Though tongue-and-groove boards are nominally the same sizes as square-edged boards, the edge joint reduces their floor coverage by about 12mm (½in) per board.

In some old buildings you may find floorboards bearing the marks left by an adze on their undersides. Such old boards have usually been trimmed to a required thickness only where they sit over the joists.

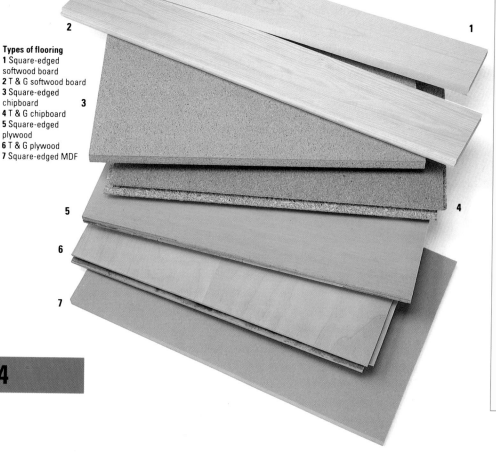

SHEET FLOORING

Softwood and hardwood boards not only provide a tough flooring; when sealed and polished they will also take on an attractive colour. Sheet materials such as flooring-grade plywood or particle boards are merely functional, however, and are usually used as a sub-base for other floor surfaces.

Plywood
Any exterior-grade plywood – known as WPB bonded plywood – can be used for flooring. Those sold as flooring-grade boards are square-edged or tongued and grooved on all four edges.

Plywood flooring laid directly over the joists should be 16 to 18mm (⅝ to ¾in) thick, though boards laid over an existing floor surface (to level it or to provide an underlay for tiles) can be 6 to 12mm (¼ to ½in) in thickness. Plywood floors are laid in the same way as chipboard ones.

Chipboard
Chipboard is a commonly available particle board made from bonded chips of wood. Only proper flooring-grade chipboard, which is compressed to a higher density than standard material, should be used for flooring. It is available in square-edged and tongue-and-groove boards. The square-edged boards measure 2.4 x 1.22m (8 x 4ft) and are 18mm (¾in) thick. Tongue-and-groove boards are available in two grades: flooring-standard and moisture-resistant. Both grades come in sheets measuring 2.4m x 600mm (8 x 2ft) and 22mm (⅞in) thick. The moisture-resistant type should always be used where damp conditions may occur, such as in bathrooms or kitchens.

The 18mm (¾in) thick boards are suitable for laying on joists spaced no more than 400mm (1ft 4in) apart. Where the joists are at 600mm (2ft) intervals, 22mm (⅞in) boarding should be used.

Medium-density fibreboard
Medium-density fibreboard (MDF) is a dense sheet material made from fine compressed wood fibres. It is produced in standard, moisture-resistant and exterior grades, and is suitable for flooring where a plain, smooth finish is required. Available in 2.4 x 1.22m (8 x 4ft) square-edged sheets in a wide range of thicknesses, it is more expensive than chipboard.

TONGUE-AND-GROOVE BOARDING

Check whether your floorboards are tongued and grooved by trying to push a knife into the gap between them.

To lift a tongue-and-groove board it is necessary first to cut through the tongue on each side of the board. Saw carefully along the line of the joint with a dovetail or tenon saw (1) held at a shallow angle. A straight wooden batten temporarily nailed along the edge of the floorboard may help you to keep the saw on a straight line.

With the tongue cut through, saw across the board and lift it as you would a plain square-edged one.

If the original flooring has been 'secret nailed' (2), use lost-head nails (3) to fix the boards back in place and conceal the nail heads with a matching wood filler.

1 Saw along the line of the joint

2 Secret-nailed boards

3 Use lost-head nails

REFITTING A CUT BOARD

The butted ends of floorboards normally meet over a joist (1). A board that has been cut flush with the side of a joist must be supported from below when it is replaced (2).

Cut a piece of 50 x 50mm (2 x 2in) softwood and screw it to the side of the joist, flush with the top edge. Screw the end of the floorboard to the support.

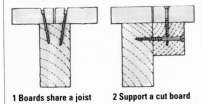

1 Boards share a joist   **2 Support a cut board**

Floorboarding is produced in lengths that are intended to run from wall to wall. In practice this rarely happens because odd, shorter lengths are often laid to save on materials. When lifting floorboards, start with these shorter pieces if possible. In many older homes one or two boards will probably have been lifted already for access to services.

Square-edged boards

Tap the blade of a bolster into the gap between the boards close to the cut end (1). Lever up the edge of the board, but try not to crush the one next to it. Fit the bolster into the gap at the other side of the board and repeat the procedure.

1 Lever up board with bolster chisel

Ease the end of the board up in this way, then work the claw of a hammer under it until there is room to slip a cold chisel under the board (2). Lift the next pair of nails, proceeding in the same fashion along the board until it is free.

2 Place cold chisel under board

Lifting a continuous board

Floorboards are nailed in place before the skirting boards are fixed, so the ends of a continuous board are trapped under them. You will have to cut the board in half before you can lift it.

Prise up the centre of the floorboard with a bolster until you can slip a cold chisel under it to keep it bowed. Remove the nails and, with a tenon saw, cut through the board (1) over the centre of the joist. You can then lift the two halves of the board, using the method described above.

A board that is too stiff to be bowed upwards, or is tongued and grooved, will have to be sawn *in situ*. This means cutting it flush with the side of the joist instead of over its centre.

Locate the side of the joist by passing the blade of a padsaw (2) vertically into the gaps on both sides of the board (the joints of tongue-and-grooved boards will also have to be cut beforehand). Mark both edges of the board where the blade stops, and draw a line between these points representing the side of the joist. Make an access slot for the padsaw blade by drilling three or four 3mm (⅛in) diameter holes close together near one end of the line marked across the surface.

Work the tip of the blade into the hole and start making the cut with short strokes. Gradually tilt the blade to a shallow angle to avoid cutting into any cables or pipes that may be hidden below. Lever up the board with a bolster chisel as described above.

Freeing the end of a board

To release the end of a floorboard that is trapped under the skirting, lift the board until it is almost vertical, then pull it straight out of the gap between the skirting and the joist (1).

A floorboard that runs beneath a partition wall must be cut close to the skirting before you can raise it (2). Drill an access hole so that you can insert the blade of a padsaw.

Alternatively, you can hire a special saw (3) that can be used for cutting floorboards. It has a curved cutting edge that allows you to saw through a board without lifting it completely.

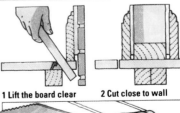

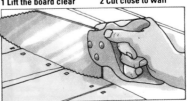

1 Lift the board clear   **2 Cut close to wall**

3 Hire a floorboard saw if necessary

1 Saw across the board

2 Find the joist's side

RE-LAYING
A FLOOR

Though floors take more wear and tear than any other interior surface, it is usually fire damage, timber decay – which would also affect the joists – or simply large gaps in the boarding caused by shrinkage that require the floor to be re-laid, or even entirely renewed.

If the floor is to be renewed, measure the room and buy your materials in advance. Leave floorboards or sheet materials to acclimatize – ideally in the room where they are to be laid – for at least a week before fixing.

● **Closing gaps**
You can re-lay floorboards without removing all the boards at once. Lift and renail about six boards at a time as you work across the floor. Finally cut and fit a new board to fill the last gap.

Removing the flooring

To lift the complete flooring you must first remove the skirting boards from the walls. If you intend to re-lay the boards, number them with chalk before starting to raise them. Lift the first few boards as described, starting from one side of the room, then prise up the remainder by working a bolster chisel between the joists and the undersides of the boards. When lifting tongue-and-groove boards, carefully ease them up two or three at a time to avoid breaking the joints, then pull them apart.

Pull all the nails out of the boards and joists, and scrape any accumulated dirt from the tops of the joists. Clean the edges of the boards similarly if they are to be reused. Check all timbers for rot or insect infestation and treat or repair them as required.

Laying floorboards
Working from a platform of loose boards, proceed in the following order.
1 Fix the first board parallel to the wall.
2 Cut and lay up to six boards, clamp them together and nail.
3 Lay the next group of boards in the same way, continue across the floor and cut the last board to fit.

Laying new floorboards

Though these instructions describe the fixing of tongue-and-groove boarding, the basic method applies equally to square-edged floorboarding.

First lay a few loose floorboards together to act as a work platform. Measure the width or the length of the room – whichever is at right angles to the joists – and cut your boards to stop 9mm (⅜in) short of the walls at each end. Lay four to six boards at a time.

Where two shorter floorboards are to be butted end to end, cut them so that the joint will be centred over a joist, but it pays to arrange several boards so that you are not left with butt joints occurring side by side.

Fix the first board with its grooved edge no more than 9mm (⅜in) from the wall and nail it in place with cut floor brads or lost-head nails that are at least twice as long as the thickness of the board.

Place the nails in pairs, one about 25mm (1in) from each edge of the board and centred on the joists. Use a nail punch to drive them about 2mm (1/16in) below the surface. When 'secret nailing', drive nails diagonally through the tongued edge instead.

Lay the other cut boards in place and clamp them up to the fixed one so as to close the edge joints. Special floorboard cramps can be hired for this, but wedges cut from 400mm (1ft 4in) offcuts of board will work just as well **(1)**. To clamp the boards with wedges, temporarily nail another floorboard just less than a board's width away from them. Insert pairs of wedges in the gap, resting on every fourth or fifth joist, and with two hammers tap the wedges toward each other. Nail the clamped floorboards in place as before, then remove the wedges and repeat the procedure with the next group of boards, continuing in this way across the room.

At the far wall, cut the last board to fit by removing the tongued edge. It should be cut to leave a gap equal to the width of the tongue or 9mm (⅜in), whichever is less. If you cannot slide the groove onto the tongue, cut away the bottom section of the grooved edge so that it will drop into place **(2)**.

1 Make wedges to clamp boards

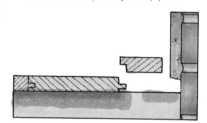
2 Cut away part of the last board's grooved edge

FLOORBOARD CRAMP

This special tool automatically grips the joist over which it is placed by means of two toothed cams. A screw-operated ram applies pressure to the floorboards when the tommy bar is turned.

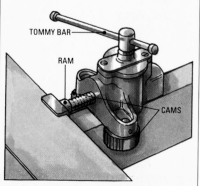
TOMMY BAR
RAM
CAMS
Hire a special cramp to re-lay floorboards

FLOORS
CHIPBOARD

LAYING
CHIPBOARD
FLOORING

SEE ALSO

For a floor that is going to be invisible beneath some kind of covering – vinyl, cork, fitted carpet or whatever – chipboard is an excellent material. It can be laid relatively quickly and is much cheaper than an equivalent amount of timber flooring. It comes square-edged or tongued and grooved. Each has its own laying technique.

CUTTING TO FIT

Square-edged boards
The widths of the boards may have to be cut down (1) so that their long edges will butt on the joists' centre lines.

Tongue-and-groove boards
Only the last boards need cutting in order to fit against the wall (2).

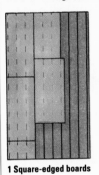

1 Square-edged boards　　**2 T&G boards**

Square-edged boards

All the edges of square-edged sheet flooring must be supported. Lay the boards with their long edges along the joists and nail 75 x 50mm (3 x 2in) softwood noggings between the joists to support the ends of the boards. The noggings against the wall can be inserted in advance; those supporting joints between boards must be nailed into place as the boards are laid.

Start with a full-length board in one corner and lay a row of boards the length of the room, cutting the last one to fit as required. Leave an expansion gap of about 9mm (⅜in) between the outer edges of the boards and the walls. The boards' inner edges should fall on the centre line of a joist. If necessary cut the boards to width, but remove the waste from the edges closest to the wall, preserving the machine-cut edges to make neat butt joints with the next row of boards. Nail down the boards, using 50mm (2in) ring-shank nails spaced about 300mm (1ft) apart along the joists and noggings. Place the nails about 18mm (¾in) from the board edges.

Cut and lay the remainder of the boards with the end joints staggered on alternate rows.

Tongue-and-groove boards

Tongue-and-groove boards are laid with their long edges running across the joists. Noggings are required only to support the outer edges of the boards close to the walls. The ends of the boards are supported by joists.

Working from one corner, lay the first board with its grooved edges about 9mm (⅜in) from the walls and nail it in place. Apply PVA wood adhesive to the joint along the end of the first board, then lay the next one in the row. Knock it up to the first board with a hammer for a good close joint, protecting the edge with a piece of scrap wood. Nail the board down as before, then wipe any surplus adhesive from the surface before it sets, using a damp rag.

Continue in this way across the floor, gluing all of the joints as you go. Cut boards to fit at the ends of rows or to fall on the centre of a joist, and stagger end joints on alternate rows.

Finally, fit the skirting boards, which will cover the expansion gaps around the perimeter of the floor.

If you wish to, you can seal the surface of the chipboard with two coats of clear polyurethane varnish to protect it from dirt.

1 Square-edged boards
Lay the boards with their long edges resting on a joist and their ends supported by noggings.

2 Tongue-and-groove boards
Lay boards crosswise with their ends falling on a joist.

1 Arrangement for laying square-edged boards

2 Arrangement for laying T&G boards

FLOOR JOISTS

Fitting services
1 Make holes for cables within the red line.
2 Place notches for pipes within red area

Accommodating pipes
Drill and saw notches for pipes and cover them with a protector.

Repairing a joist
The stages for replacing a joist are combined in the illustration.
1 Cut away old joist.
2 Cut out wall plate.
3 Fit new wall plate.
4 Cut and fit new joist and brace the joint with bolted joist timbers.

As all floor joists are loadbearing, their size and spacing in new structures must satisfy a Building Control Officer. However, for most domestic repairs calculations are not usually necessary – matching new timber for old should suffice.

Use 'structurally graded' timber, which has been expertly examined or machine-tested. SS is the grade mark of 'special structural timber', used for joists; GS, 'general structural timber', is for general framing as well as joists. Purple colour-coded MSS and green MGS denote machine-graded timber to the same specification.

Fitting services

Service runs like heating pipes and electric cables can run in the void below a suspended ground floor, but those running at right angles to the joists in upper floors must pass through the joists, which are covered by flooring above and a ceiling below.

So as not to weaken the structure, bore holes for cables through the centre of a joist, or at least 50mm (2in) below the top edge to clear floor nails. Try to place the holes within the middle two-thirds of the joist's length (**1**).

Notches for pipe runs in the top edge should ideally be no deeper than one-eighth the depth of the joist and within a quarter of the joist's length at each end (**2**). Make a notch by drilling through the joist, then saw down to the hole.

Repairing joists

Floor joists which have been seriously attacked by wet rot, dry rot or insect infestation have to be cut out and replaced. Such attack usually occurs at ground-floor level because of its proximity to the damp soil. If the damage is extensive, or the upper floors are also affected, you should call in an expert to do the job. However, if it is localized and not too serious you can probably deal with it yourself.

Remove the skirtings and lift the floorboards over the infected area until you reach a sleeper wall. Test the condition of the wood – joists, floorboards and skirting boards – by spiking it with a sharp knife. If the blade penetrates easily the wood will have to be replaced. Sound wood can be treated with chemical preserver to kill rot spores or woodworm larvae.

Preparation
The damp conditions which have caused the outbreak of wet or dry rot must themselves be identified and corrected before any remedial work on the timbers is carried out.

All infected timbers must be removed in an area extending at least 450mm (1ft 6in) beyond the last visible signs of attack, and all surrounding masonry must be treated with a fungicide. Burn all the infected timber. The following assumes that the end of a joist and perhaps also the wall plate are affected.

Saw through and remove the infected end of the joist, cutting it back to the centre of the nearest sleeper wall. If the wall plate which has been supporting the joist is also affected, cut it away. If the wall plate is built into the brickwork, drill a series of holes into its edge and finish cutting it away with a wood chisel and mallet, trimming the remaining ends square. Wall plates on sleeper walls can be cut with a saw.

Replacement
Cut a new length of wall-plate timber to fill the gap and treat it thoroughly with wood preserver.

If the original mortar bed joint and damp-proof course are undamaged, apply a coating of liquid bituminous damp-proofing over it and put the new section of wall plate into place.

If necessary, re-lay the bed joint and insert a new length of DPC, making sure that its ends overlap the ends of the old one, if present, by at least 150mm (6in). Then reseat the wall plate.

Now cut a length of new joist to sit on the repaired wall plate and meet the cut end of the old joist on the sleeper wall. Treat it well with timber preserver. To ensure that it is level with the other joists, trim its underside or pack it with DPC felt.

Brace the joint with two 900mm (3ft) lengths of joist timber – also treated – on each side and bolt through with four coach bolts and two timber connectors for each bolt.

Finally, replace all the floorboards and skirtings.

FITTING JOIST HANGERS

Sections of infected wall plate which have had to be removed can be replaced with metal joist hangers to support the ends of the repaired joists.

Having removed the damaged joist and section of wall plates (see above), lay bricks in the resulting slot. Before laying the mortar, check on the condition of the DPC and reinforce it with an extra layer of DPC felt or a liquid damp-proofing material if you think it necessary.

Set the flange of the joist hanger in mortar at the required level, then allow the mortar to harden before fitting the new section of joist as indicated above.

Skirtings are protective 'kick boards', usually moulded to form a decorative border between the floor and walls. Modern skirtings are relatively small and simply formed, with a rounded or bevelled top edge.

Skirtings found in older houses can be as much as 300mm (1ft) wide and quite elaborately moulded, but those in most homes are about 175mm (7in) wide and of 'ovolo' or 'torus' design. These can still be bought from timber merchants. Some will supply more elaborate designs to special order. Skirtings can be nailed directly on to plastered brickwork or to battens, known as 'grounds', which have been fixed during the plastering stage. Skirting boards on partition walls are nailed to timber studs.

Removing the skirting

Remove a skirting by levering it away from the wall with a crowbar or bolster chisel. Where a skirting butts against a door architrave or an external corner it can be levered off easily enough, but a continuous length whose ends are mitred into internal corners may have to be cut before it can be removed.

Tap the blade of the bolster between the skirting and the wall, and lever the top edge away sufficiently to insert the chisel end of the crowbar behind it. Place a thin strip of wood behind the crowbar to protect the wall, then tap the bolster in again a little to one side, working along the skirting in this way as

the nails loosen until the board is free.

With the board removed, pull the nails out through the back of the skirting to avoid splitting the face.

Cutting a long skirting

A long stretch of skirting may bend sufficiently for you to cut it in place. Lever it away at its centre and insert blocks of wood (1), one on each side of the proposed cut, to hold the board about 25mm (1in) from the wall.

Make a vertical cut with a panel saw held at about 45 degrees to the face of the board (2) and work with short strokes, using the tip of the saw.

Fitting new skirting

A damaged skirting should be restored if possible, particularly if it is an unusual moulding for which there is no modern replacement; otherwise you could try making one up yourself from various moulded sections (see right). Standard mouldings are readily available.

Measure the length of each wall, bearing in mind that most skirtings are mitred at the corners.

Mark the length on the plain bottom edge of the skirting board, mark a 45-degree angle for the mitre, and extend the marked line across the face of the board, using a try square. Clamp the board on edge in a vice and carefully saw down the line at that angle.

Sometimes moulded skirting boards are scribed and butt-jointed at internal corners. To achieve the required profile, cut the end off one board at 45 degrees as for a mitre joint (1) and, with a coping saw, cut along the contour line on the moulded face so that it will 'jig-saw' with its neighbour (2).

Fix skirting boards with cut-clasp nails or masonry nails when nailing to brickwork, but use lost-head nails when attaching a skirting to wooden grounds or stud partitions.

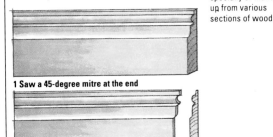

Making a skirting
If you are unable to buy a length of skirting to match your original, have one machined specially or make one up from various sections of wood.

1 Prise skirting away from wall and pack out

2 Cut through skirting with tip of saw

1 Saw a 45-degree mitre at the end

2 Cut the shape following the contour line

SKIRTING MOULDINGS

Most standard skirting mouldings are made in softwood ready for painting. Hardwood is not so common and is usually reserved for special decorative skirtings. Hardwoods are coated with a clear finish. 'Moulded-reverse' skirtings are machined with a different profile on each side of the board.

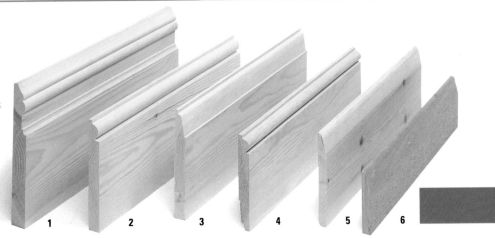

Selection of skirting mouldings
1 Bolection mould skirting 2 Torus skirting
3 Ovolo skirting 4 Torus/ovolo reverse skirting
5 Bevelled/rounded reverse skirting 6 Bevelled hardwood skirting

1   2   3   4   5   6

DOORS: TYPES AND CONSTRUCTION

At first glance there appears to be a great variety of doors to choose from, but in fact most of the differences are simply stylistic. They are all based on a small number of construction methods.

The wide range of styles can sometimes tempt householders into buying doors that are inappropriate for the houses they live in. When replacing a front door you should be careful to choose one that is not incongruous with the architectural style of your house.

Buying a door

Internal and external doors in softwood and hardwood are available, the latter being the more expensive and normally reserved for special rooms or entrances where the natural features of the wood can be appreciated. Softwood doors are for more general workaday use and are intended to be painted. However, some people prefer a clear finish.

Glazed doors are often used for front and rear entrances. Traditionally, these are of wooden-frame construction, though modern aluminium-framed and uPVC plastic doors can be bought in standard sizes, complete with double glazing and fitments.

Wooden-frame and panel doors are supplied in unfinished wood, and mostly require trimming, glazing and fitting out with hinges, locks and letter plates.

Door sizes

Doors are made in several standard sizes to meet most domestic needs. The range of heights is usually 2m (6ft 6in), 2.03m (6ft 8in) and occasionally 2.17m (7ft). Widths range from 600mm (2ft) to 900mm (3ft) in steps of about 75mm (3in). Thicknesses vary from 35mm (1⅜in) to 44mm (1¾in).

Older houses often have relatively large doors to the main rooms on the ground floor, but modern homes tend to have standard-size joinery throughout. The standard is usually 2m x 762mm (6ft 6in x 2ft 6in), except for front-entrance doors which are invariably larger in order to harmonize with the proportions of the façade.

When replacing a door in an old house, where the openings may well be of non-standard sizes, have a door made to measure or buy one of the nearest available size and trim it to fit, removing an equal amount from each edge to preserve the frame's symmetry.

External flush door
A central rail is fitted to take a letter plate.

Planted moulding

Bolection moulding

Panel doors

Panel doors have hardwood or softwood frames made with mortise and tenons or dowel joints. The frames are rebated or grooved to house the panels, which can be of solid wood, plywood or glass. Cheaper doors, constructed from moulded-hardboard panels fixed to a lightweight frame, are also available.

1 Muntins
These are the central vertical members of the door. They are jointed into the three cross rails.

2 Panels
These may be of solid wood or of plywood. They are held loosely in grooves in the frame to allow for shrinkage without splitting. They stiffen the door.

3 Cross rails
Top, centre and bottom rails are tenoned into the stiles. In cheaper doors the mortise-and-tenon joints are replaced with dowel joints.

4 Stiles
These are the upright members at the sides of the door. They carry the hinges and door locks.

Panel-door mouldings
The frame's inner edges may be plain or moulded to form a decorative border. Small mouldings are machined on the frame before assembly or pinned to the inside edge. An ordinary planted moulding (see far left) can shrink away from the frame, making cracks in the paintwork. A bolection moulding which laps the frame overcomes this problem.

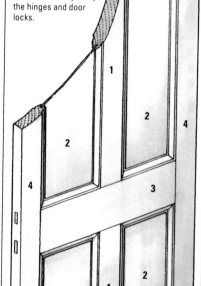

Panel door

Flush doors

Flush doors have softwood frames faced on both sides with sheets of plywood or hardboard, and infilled with a core material. Used mainly internally, they are lightweight, cheap and simple, but lacking in character. External flush doors have a central rail to take a letter plate. Firecheck doors are a special fire-retardant grade.

1 Top and bottom rails
These are tenoned into the stiles (side pieces).

2 Intermediate rails
These lighter rails, jointed to the stiles, are notched to allow the passage of air to prevent the panels sinking.

3 Lock blocks
A softwood block to take a mortise lock is glued to each stile.

4 Panels
The plywood or hardboard panels are left plain for painting or finished with a wood veneer. Metal-skinned doors may be ordered specially.

Core material
Paper or cardboard honeycomb is usually sandwiched between the panels. A solid fire-retardant material forms the core of firecheck doors.

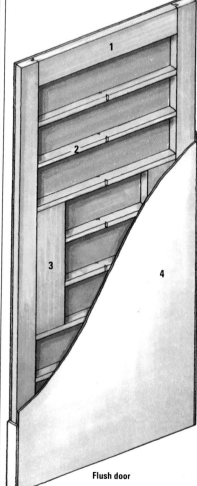

Flush door

Ledged and braced doors

These doors have a rustic look and are often found in old houses, outbuildings and garden walls. They are strong, secure and cheap, though sometimes a little crude. A superior framed version is tenon-jointed or dowelled instead of being merely nailed or stapled.

1 Battens
Tongue-and-groove boards are nailed to the ledges.

2 T-hinges
Butt hinges will not hold in the end-grain of the ledges, so long T-hinges take the weight.

3 Braces
These diagonals, notched into the ledges, transmit the weight to the hinges and stop the door sagging.

4 Ledges
These are the cross rails to which the battens are nailed.

Framed, ledged, braced and battened door

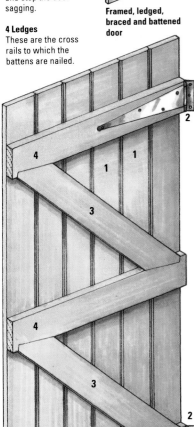

Ledged, braced and battened door

DOORFRAMES AND CASINGS

External frames

An exterior door is typically fitted into a wooden frame consisting of the head (1) at the top, the sill (2), with a water-repellent weather bar, at the bottom and, mortised and tenoned between them, two rebated side posts (3).

The horns, 50mm (2in) projections (4) of the head on each side, support the joints and are built into the brickwork to hold the frame in place. The pallets (5) are wooden plates, also built into the brickwork, for nail-fixing the frame.

Metal brackets (6) can provide an alternative way of fixing the doorframe.

Aluminium and uPVC door sets are supplied with an extruded frame and separate sill. The components are fixed to the masonry with frame fixings, and the doorframe to the sill with self-tapping screws.

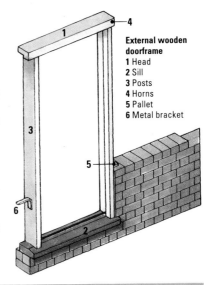

External wooden doorframe
1 Head
2 Sill
3 Posts
4 Horns
5 Pallet
6 Metal bracket

Internal casings

Internal doors are hung in a timber lining frame (see below) made up from three members: the soffit casing (1) at the top and jamb casings (2) on both sides of the opening. They are jointed together at the corners with bare-faced tongue-and-groove joints (3). The jamb casings are nailed to pallets, wooden plugs (4) in the brickwork, at 600mm (2ft) intervals. Casings may also be nail-fixed directly to block walls. An architrave (5) covers the joints between the casings and wall. The door closes against applied doorstops (6) which form a rebate.

In better-quality buildings hardwood casings are often nailed to softwood grounds (see below). These are rough-sawn lengths of timber which are nailed in place to form a frame around the door opening. The soffit grounds (7) are nailed to the front of the lintel and the jamb grounds (8) to wooden plugs in the brickwork. The grounds provide a level for the wall plaster and a good fixing for the architrave moulding.

Internal door casing
1 Soffit casing
2 Jamb casing
3 Bare-faced T&G joint
4 Pallet
5 Architrave
6 Doorstop

Internal hardwood casing
7 Soffit grounds
8 Jamb grounds

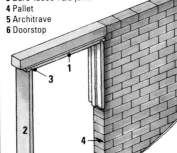
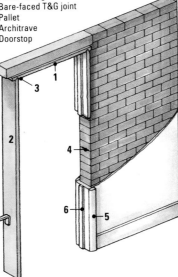
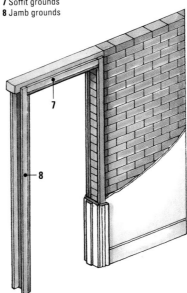

FITTING AND HANGING DOORS

Whatever the style of door you wish to fit the procedure is similar, with only minor differences to contend with. Two good-quality 100mm (4in) butt hinges are enough to support a standard door, but if you are hanging a fire door or a heavy hardwood one you should add a third, central hinge.

As you will have to try a door in its frame several times to get the perfect fit, it pays to have someone working with you.

Fitting a door

Before attaching the hinges to a new door make sure that it fits nicely into its frame. It should have a clearance of 2mm (1⁄16in) at the top and sides and should clear the floor by at least 6mm (1⁄4in). As much as 12mm (1⁄2in) may be required for a carpeted floor.

Measure the height and width of the door opening and the depth of the rebate in the frame into which the door must fit. Choose a door of the right thickness and, if you cannot get one that fits the opening exactly, select one large enough to be trimmed down.

Cutting to size

New doors are often supplied with 'horns', extensions to their stiles which prevent the corners being damaged while the doors are in storage. Cut these off with a saw (1) before starting to trim the door to size.

Transfer the measurements from the opening to the door, making allowance for necessary clearances all round.

To reduce the width of the door support it on edge, latch-stile up, in a portable bench, then plane the stile down to the marked line. If a lot of wood has to be removed, take some off each stile– this is especially important in the case of panel doors in order to preserve their symmetry.

If you need to take off more than 6mm (1⁄4in) to reduce the height of the door, remove it with a saw and finish off with a plane. Otherwise plane the waste off (2). The plane must be extremely sharp to deal with the end grain of the stiles. Work from each corner towards the centre of the bottom rail to avoid 'chipping out' the corners.

Try the door in the frame, supporting it on shallow wedges (3). If it still does not fit take it down and remove more wood where appropriate.

1 Saw off horns

2 Plane to size

3 Wedge the door

Fitting hinges

The upper hinge is set about 175mm (7in) from the door's top edge and the lower one about 250mm (10in) from the bottom. They are cut equally into the stile and doorframe. Wedge the door in its opening and, with the wedges tapped in to raise it to the right floor clearance, mark the positions of the hinges on both the door and frame.

Stand the door on edge, hinge stile uppermost, open a hinge and, with its knuckle projecting from the edge of the door, align it with the marks and draw round the flap with a pencil (1). Set a marking gauge to the thickness of the flap and mark the depth of the housing. With a chisel, make a series of shallow cuts across the grain (2) and pare out the waste to the scored line. Repeat the procedure with the second hinge, then, using the flaps as guides, drill pilot holes for the screws and fix both hinges into their housings.

Wedge the door in the open position, aligning the free hinge flaps with the marks on the doorframe. Make sure that the knuckles of the hinges are parallel with the frame, then trace the housings on the frame (3) and cut them out as you did the others.

Adjusting and aligning

Hang the door with one screw holding each hinge and see if it closes smoothly. If the latch stile rubs on the frame you may have to make one or both housings slightly deeper. If the door appears to strain against the hinges it is said to be 'hinge bound'. In this case insert thin cardboard beneath the hinge flaps to pack them out. When the door finally opens and closes properly drive in the rest of the screws.

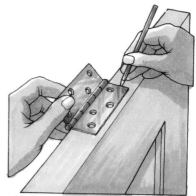

1 Mark round the flap with a pencil

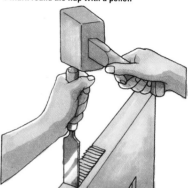

2 Cut across the grain with a chisel

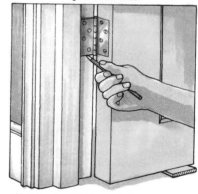

3 Mark the size of the flap on the frame

MEASUREMENTS

A door that fits well will open and close freely and look symmetrical in the frame. Use the figures given as a guide for trimming the door and setting out the position of the hinges.

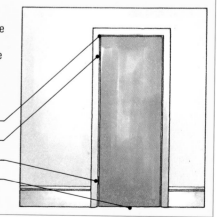

2mm (1⁄16in) clearance at top and sides

Upper hinge 175mm (7in) from the top

Lower hinge 250mm (10in) from the bottom

6 to 12mm (1⁄4 to 1⁄2in) gap at the bottom

CLEARANCE AND WEATHER- PROOFING

SEE ALSO

Details for:
Door construction   60

Rising butt hinges

Rising butt hinges lift a door as it is opened and are fitted to prevent it dragging on thick pile carpet.

They are made in two parts: a flap with a fixed pin which is screwed to the doorframe, and another flap with a single knuckle which is fixed to the door. The knuckle pivots on the pin.

Rising butt hinges must be fixed one way up only, and are therefore made specifically for left-hand or right-hand opening. The countersunk screwholes in the fixed-pin flap indicate the side to which it is made to be fitted.

Fitting

Trim the door and mark the hinge positions (see opposite), but before fitting the hinges plane a shallow bevel at the top outer corner of the hinge stile so that it will clear the frame as it opens. As the stile runs through to the top of the door, plane from the outer corner towards the centre to avoid splitting the wood. The top strip of the doorstop will mask the bevel when the door is closed.

Fit the hinges to the door and frame, then lower the door on to the hinge pins, taking care not to damage the architrave above the opening.

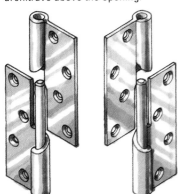

Left-hand opening   **Right-hand opening**

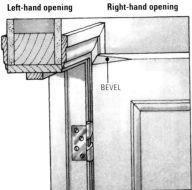

Plane a shallow bevel to clear the doorframe

Weatherproofing a door

Fitting a weatherboard

A weatherboard is a special moulding which is fitted to the bottom of an external door to shed rainwater away from the threshold. To fit one, measure the width of the opening between the doorstops and cut the moulding to fit, cutting one end at a slight angle where it meets the doorframe on the latch side. This will allow it to clear the frame as the door swings open.

Use screws and a waterproof glue to attach a weatherboard to an unpainted door. When fitting one to a door that is already finished, apply a thick coat of primer to the back surface of the weatherboard to make a weatherproof seal, then screw the moulding in place while the primer is still wet. Fill or plug the screw holes before you prime and finish the weatherboard.

Allowing for a weather bar

Though a rebate cut into the head and side posts of an external doorframe provides a seal round an inward-opening door, a rebate cut into the sill at the foot of the door would merely encourage water to flow into the house.

Unless protected by a porch, a door in an exposed position needs to be fitted with a weather bar to prevent rainwater running underneath. This is a metal or plastic strip which is set into the step or sill. If you are putting in a new door and wish to fit a weather bar, use a router or power saw to cut a rebate across the bottom of the door in order to clear the bar.

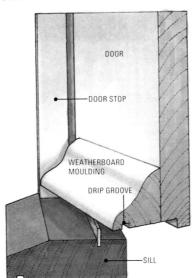

Door fitted with a weatherboard

ADJUSTING BUTT HINGES

Perhaps you have a door catching on a bump in the floor as it opens. You can, of course, fit rising butt hinges, but the problem can be overcome by resetting the lower hinge so that its knuckle projects slightly more than the top one. The door will still hang vertically when closed, but as it opens the out-of-line pins will throw it upwards so that the bottom edge will clear the bump.

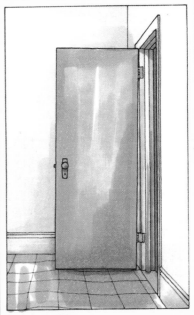

Resetting the hinge
You may have to reset both hinges to the new angle to prevent binding.

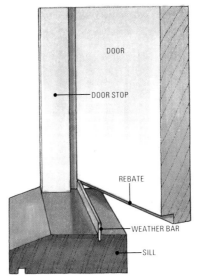

Sill fitted with weather bar

63

RENEWING A DOORFRAME

External doorframes are built into the brickwork as it is erected, so replacing one inevitably damages the plaster or rendering.

In older houses the frames are recessed into the brickwork, the inside face of the frame flush with the plasterwork and the architrave covering the joint. Modern houses may have frames close to or flush with the outer face of the brickwork. Work from whichever side the frame is closer to.

Measure the door and buy a standard frame to fit, or make one from standard frame sections.

Removing the old frame

Chop back the plaster or rendering with a chisel to expose the back face of the doorframe **(1)**.

With a universal saw **(2)** cut through the three metal fixings holding the frame in the brickwork on each side, one about 225mm (9in) from both the top and bottom and one halfway up.

Saw through the jambs halfway up **(3)**, and if necessary cut the head member and the sill. Lever the frame members out with a crowbar.

Clear any loose material from the opening and repair a vertical DPC in a cavity wall with gun-applied mastic to keep moisture out of the gap between inner and outer layers of brickwork.

Fitting the new frame

Fitting a frame is easier with its horns removed, but this weakens it. If possible fit the frame with horns shaped like the old ones (see right).

Wedge the frame in position, checking that it is central, square and plumb. Drill three counterbored clearance holes in each jamb for the fixing screws, positioned about 300mm (1ft) from the top and bottom with one halfway. Try to avoid drilling into mortar joints. Run a masonry drill through the clearance holes to mark their positions on the brickwork.

Remove the frame, drill the holes in the brickwork and insert No12 wall plugs. Replace the frame and fix it with 100mm (4in) No12 steel screws. Plug the counterbored holes. Alternatively, use nailable-plug frame fixings.

Pack any gap under the sill with mortar. Make good the brickwork, rendering or plasterwork and apply mastic sealant round the outer edge of the frame to seal any small gaps.

When fitting an aluminium or uPVC frame, first level the sill on a bed of mortar and screw-fix it in place. Insert and plumb the frame, then fasten it to the walls and sill. Seal all the joints with frame sealant.

1 Cut back to expose the back of the frame

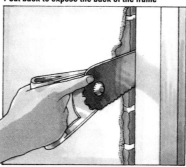
2 Cut through the frame fixings

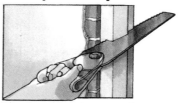
3 Saw through the frame to remove it

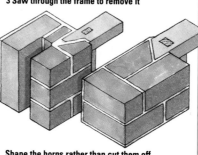
Shape the horns rather than cut them off

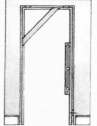
Screw the frame to the plugged wall

FIXING A DOOR CASING

A new internal door opening will need a casing to finish it. These are usually of board, 25mm (1in) thick where the applied doorstop is used or 38mm (1½in) when rebated to take the door. The width of the casing should equal the thickness of the finished wall.

Door casings are sold by joinery suppliers as unassembled kits for standard door sizes. If your door is not standard you can make a lining, using a bare-faced tongue-and-groove joint **(1)**.

Wedge the assembled and braced frame in position in the opening **(2)** and, if necessary, place hardboard or plywood packing between the lintel and the soffit casing at each end. Check that the edges project equally from both faces of the wall and nail the soffit casing with two 75mm (3in) oval nails.

Plumb one jamb casing with a straightedge and spirit level, then pack it in place **(3)**. Start nailing about 75mm (3in) from the bottom and work upwards, checking for true as you go. Place the nails in pairs 450mm (1ft 6in) apart.

Cut a 'pinch rod' to fit closely between the jamb casings at the top of the frame, then place it across the bottom and pack out the unfixed jamb to fit **(4)**. Check that the jamb is plumb. Nail the casing in place and use the pinch rod to check the distance between the jamb casings at all levels.

Finish the wall surface round the opening and cover the joint with a mitred architrave moulding. Hang the door and fit the doorstop battens to the inside of the casing.

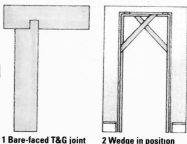
1 Bare-faced T&G joint   **2 Wedge in position**

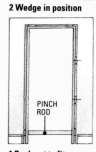
3 Plumb on jamb   **4 Pack out to fit**

PINCH ROD

The great majority of external doorframes are constructed of softwood, and this, if it is regularly maintained with a good paint system, will give years of excellent service. However, the ends of door sills and the frame posts are vulnerable to wet rot if they are subject to continual wetting. This can happen when the frame has moved because the timber has shrunk, or where old pointing has fallen out and left a gap where water can penetrate. Alternatively, old and porous brickwork or an ineffective damp-proof course can be the cause of wet-rot damage.

Prevention is always better than cure, so check round the frame for any gaps and apply a mastic sealant where necessary. Keep all pointing in good order. A minor outbreak of wet rot can be treated with the aid of a proprietary repair kit and a chemical preserver.

It is possible for the sill to rot without the doorposts being affected, in which case just replace the sill. But if the posts are also affected, repair them at the same time (see right). In some cases the post ends are tenoned into the sill and fitted as a unit.

Replacing a sill

You can buy 150 x 50mm (6 x 2in) softwood or hardwood door-sill sections which can be cut to the required length. If your sill is not of a standard-shaped section, you can have a replacement made to order. A hardwood such as oak will be relatively expensive, but will prove more economical in the long run as it lasts much longer.

Taking out the old sill
First measure and note down the width of the door opening, then remove the door. The posts are usually tenoned into the sill, so split the sill lengthways with a wood chisel in order to dismantle the joints. A saw-cut across the centre of the sill makes the job easier.

The ends of the sill are set into the brickwork on each side of the opening. To release the sill, use a plugging chisel to chop out the mortar joints carefully, then pull out a brick from each side. Keep them for replacing later.

The new sill has to be inserted from the front so that it can be tucked under the posts and into the brickwork. Cut off the tenons level with the shoulders of the posts (1). Mark and cut shallow housings for the ends of the posts in the top of the new sill, spacing them apart as previously noted. The housings must be deep enough to take the full width of the posts (2) which may mean the sill being slightly higher than the original one, so you will have to trim a little off the bottom of the door.

Fitting a new sill
Try the new sill for fit and check that it is level. Before fixing it, apply two coats of all-purpose wood preserver to its underside and to both ends, and, as a precaution against rising or penetrating damp, apply two or three coats of bitumen latex emulsion to the brickwork in contact with the sill.

When both treatments are dry, glue the sill to the posts, using an exterior-grade woodworking adhesive. Wedge the underside of the sill with pieces of roofing slate to push it up against the ends of the doorposts. Skew-nail the posts to the sill and leave it for the adhesive to set.

Pack the gap between the underside of the sill and the masonry with a stiff mortar of 3 parts sand : 1 part cement, then rebond and point the bricks. Finish by treating the wood with a preserver and seal any gaps around the doorframe with mastic.

1 Cut tenons off level with the joint's shoulder

2 Cut a housing to receive the post

REPAIRING DOORPOSTS

Rot can attack the ends of doorposts where they meet stone steps or are set into concrete, especially in a doorway that is regularly exposed to driving rain.

If the damage is not too extensive the rotten end can be cut away and replaced with a new piece, either scarf-jointed or halving-jointed into place. If your sill is made from wood, combine the following information with that given for replacing a sill (see left).

First remove the door, then saw off the end of the affected post back to sound timber. For a scarf joint make the cut at 45 degrees to the face of the post (1); for a halving joint cut it square. If the post is located on a metal dowel set into the step, chop out the dowel with a cold chisel.

Measure and cut a matching section of post to length, allowing for the overlap of the joint, then cut the end to 45 degrees or mark and cut both parts of the post to form a halving joint (2).

Drill a hole in the end of the new section for the metal dowel if it is still usable. If not, make a new one from a piece of galvanized-steel gas pipe and prime it to prevent corrosion. Treat the new wood with a preserver and insert the dowel. Set the dowel in mortar and glue and screw the joint (3).

If a dowel is not used, fix the post to the wall with counterbored screws. Place hardboard or plywood packing behind it if necessary and plug the screw holes.

Apply a mastic sealant to the joints between the door post, wall and base.

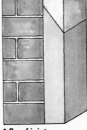

1 Scarf joint

2 Halving joint

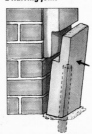

3 Set dowel in mortar as you close up either joint

REPAIRING A ROTTEN FRAME

SEE ALSO

Details for:
Door frames   61

65

WINDOWS: TYPES AND CONSTRUCTION

Traditionally, windows have been referred to as 'lights', and the term 'fixed light' is still used to describe a window or part of a frame that does not open. The section that opens for ventilation, the 'sash', is a separate frame that slides vertically or is hinged from its side, top or bottom edge. Windows of the hinged type are commonly referred to as casement windows. A pane of glass can also be pivoted horizontally as a single sash, or several can be grouped together to make up a louvre window.

Most frames and sashes are made up from moulded sections of solid wood. Mild steel and, more recently, aluminium or rigid plastic are also used, though such frames are usually fixed to the brickwork by means of wooden sub-frames.

TRANSOM
MULLION

1 Casement window

2 Glazing bars

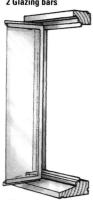

3 Steel casement type

Casement windows

Window frames with hinged sashes – casement windows – are the most common and are now produced in the widest range of materials and styles.

A traditional wooden window frame and its hinged sash are constructed in much the same way as a door and its frame. A jamb at each side is joined with mortise and tenons to the head member at the top and into a sill at the bottom (see below). The frame may be divided vertically by a 'mullion', or horizontally by a 'transom' (1).

The sash, which fits within the frame, has its top and bottom rails jointed into its side stiles. Glazing bars – relatively lightweight moulded sections – are used to sub-divide the glazed area for smaller panes (2).

Side-hung sashes are fitted on butt hinges or sometimes, for better access to the outside of the glass, on 'easy clean' extension hinges. A lever fastener, or 'cockspur', for securing the sash is screwed to the middle of the stile on the opening side, while a casement stay on the bottom rail holds the sash in various open positions and also acts as a locking device when the sash is closed. Top-hung sashes, or vents, are secured with a stay only.

Galvanized mild-steel casement windows (3) were once popular for houses and blocks of flats. They are made in the same format as wooden hinged windows, but have a slimmer framework. The joints of the metal sections are welded.

Mild-steel windows are strong and long-lasting but vulnerable to rust unless protected by galvanized plating or sound paintwork. Rusting is caused both by weathering outside and condensation on the inside.

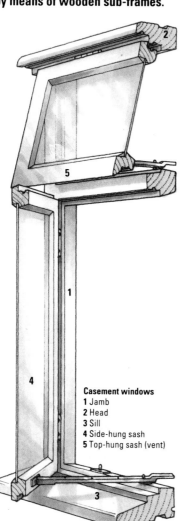

Casement windows
1 Jamb
2 Head
3 Sill
4 Side-hung sash
5 Top-hung sash (vent)

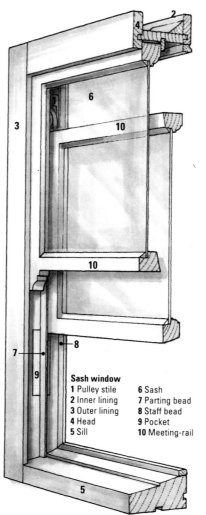

Sash window
1 Pulley stile   6 Sash
2 Inner lining   7 Parting bead
3 Outer lining   8 Staff bead
4 Head   9 Pocket
5 Sill   10 Meeting-rail

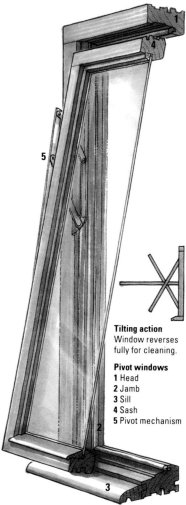

Tilting action
Window reverses fully for cleaning.

Pivot windows
1 Head
2 Jamb
3 Sill
4 Sash
5 Pivot mechanism

Sash windows

Vertically sliding windows are commonly known as sash windows. When both the top and bottom sashes can be opened they are referred to as 'double-hung' sash windows.

The traditional wooden sash window (see opposite) is constructed with a 'box frame' in which the jambs are made up from three boards: the pulley stile and the inner and outer lining. A back completes the box that houses the sash counterweights. The head is made up in a similar way but without the back lining, and the sill is of solid wood. The pulley stiles are jointed into the sill and the linings are set in a rebate.

The sashes of a double-hung window are held in tracks formed by the outer lining, a parting bead and an inner staff bead. The beads can be removed for servicing the sash mechanism. Each sash is counterbalanced by two cast-iron weights – one at each side – which are attached by strong cords or chains that pass over pulleys in the stiles. Access to the weights is through 'pockets' – removable pieces of wood – set in the lower part of the stiles.

The top sash slides in the outer track and overlaps the inner bottom sash at their horizontal 'meeting-rails'. The closing faces of the meeting-rails are bevelled, and their wedging action helps to prevent the sashes rattling. It also provides better clearance when the window is opened, and improves security when it is locked. The sashes are secured by two-part fasteners of various types fitted on the meeting-rails.

Spiral balances
Modern wooden or aluminium vertically sliding sashes have spring-assisted spiral balances which do not need a deep box construction. Rather than being concealed, the slim balances are fitted on the faces of the stiles.

Spiral balances
The balances are usually fixed to the faces of the frame stiles and set in grooves in the sash stiles.

Pivot windows

Wooden-framed pivot windows (see opposite) are constructed in a similar way to casement windows, but the sash is held on a pair of hinge mechanisms which allow the window to be tilted right over to provide for easy cleaning from inside. A safety catch is fitted which locks the frame open at 100mm (4in) and fully reversed.

Pivoting roof windows are available for pitched roofs with slopes from 15 to 90 degrees. Like the vertical pivoting windows, they can be fully reversed for cleaning. The windows are supplied double-glazed with sealed units, and ventilators are incorporated in the frame or sash. The timbers are protected on the outside by a metal covering, and flashing kits are supplied for fitting to tile or slate roofs.

Louvre windows
A louvre window is another form of pivot window. The louvres are unframed 'blades' of glass, 6mm (¼in) thick, which have their long edges ground and polished. The louvres are held at each end in moulded plastic carriers which pivot on an alloy upright member, and this is screwed to a wooden frame. One side of the window is fitted with an opening and locking mechanism which links the louvres together so that they all operate as one.

Louvre windows are effective as ventilators but they do not provide good security unless they are fitted with bonded blade locks.

Where an opening is more than 1.07m (3ft 6in) wide it is best to use two sets of louvres, with the central pair of uprights set back to back and linked with coupling blocks to form a mullion.

Use two sets of louvres for a wide opening

ALUMINIUM AND PLASTIC WINDOW FRAMES

Aluminium windows
These are often used in new houses or as replacements for old wooden or metal windows. The aluminium is extruded into complex sections (1) to hold double-glazed sealed units and draught strips and, finished in white, satin silver, black or bronze, requires no maintenance. These highly engineered windows come complete with concealed projection hinges and lockable fasteners. They need no stays to hold them open.

To combat condensation the latest designs incorporate a 'thermal break' of insulating material in the hollow sections of the frame.

Most aluminium windows designed for replacement work are purpose-made and fitted by specialist companies. They usually need wooden sub-frames.

Plastic windows
Rigid plastic windows (2) are rather similar to aluminium ones, but are thicker through their sections. They are manufactured in white plastic and once installed require no maintenance.

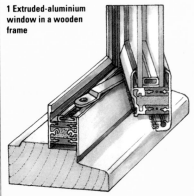

1 Extruded-aluminium window in a wooden frame

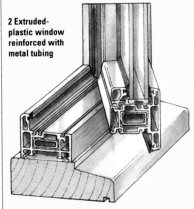

2 Extruded-plastic window reinforced with metal tubing

HOW WINDOWS ARE FITTED

Solid walls

In older houses it is usual to find the window-frame jambs set in recesses on the inside of the brickwork. The openings were formed before the windows were fitted and the frames were nailed or screwed into wooden plugs in the brickwork. No vertical damp-proof courses were fitted; evaporation was relied upon to keep the walls dry.

The frames in a 225mm (9in) thick wall were set flush with the inside. In a 340mm (1ft 1½in) wall they were set back from the inner surface. All required sub-sills, usually of stone, outside.

Brickwork above the opening in a traditional brick wall might be supported by a brick arch or a stone lintel. Flat or shallow-curved arches were generally used, their thickness being the width of one brick. Wooden lintels were placed behind them to support the rest of the wall's thickness. Semi-circular arches were usually as thick as the wall.

Many stone lintels were carved to make decorative features. As with arches, an inner lintel shared the weight. Such openings were never wide because of the relative weaknesses of the materials. The wide windows of main rooms had several openings divided by brick or stone columns.

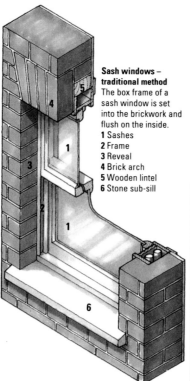

Sash windows – traditional method
The box frame of a sash window is set into the brickwork and flush on the inside.
1 Sashes
2 Frame
3 Reveal
4 Brick arch
5 Wooden lintel
6 Stone sub-sill

Cavity walls

The window frames in modern houses are usually installed while the brickwork is in the process of being erected. They are fixed into place with metal brackets known as 'frame cramps'; these are screwed to the jambs of the frame and set in the mortar bed joints. There are three such cramps on each side of the window frame.

Cavity walls must have a vertical damp-proof course. This is sandwiched between the external brick leaf of the wall and the cavity-closing bricks of the inner leaf. The window frame is set forward in the opening and covers the joint. Sometimes the damp-proof courses are fastened to the frames.

With a window frame in this position a good deal of the wall's thickness is exposed on the inside of the house. The sides of the opening, known as 'reveals', are finished off with plaster, as is the top or soffit.

The ledge at the bottom is finished with a window board which is tongued into a groove along the back of the frame sill and also screwed or nailed down to the brickwork. Quarry tiles are sometimes used to form the inner sill.

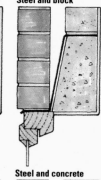

Sash windows – modern method
The brickwork is built around the window frame and includes a vertical DPC.
1 Frame
2 DPC
3 Concrete lintel
4 Wooden sill
5 Frame cramp

CONCRETE AND STEEL LINTELS

Modern lintels are made from reinforced concrete or galvanized steel or a combination of both. These extremely strong lintels can support brickwork over a considerable span, enabling large picture windows to be installed without additional support.

A damp-proof course must be provided above the window opening in order to prevent any moisture within the cavity permeating the inner leaf of masonry or the window frame, though some metal lintels can be installed without additional damp-proof material.

The front face of a concrete 'through-the-wall' or 'boot' lintel can be seen above the opening. Where a brick facing is required a steel lintel is used and the bricks are laid on the relatively thin metal edge in bonded courses or on their ends to simulate a brick arch.

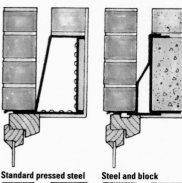

Standard pressed steel   Steel and block

Steel and wood   Steel and concrete

Through-the-wall lintel   Concrete boot lintel

Inevitably, old wooden casements and sash windows will have deteriorated to some extent, but regular maintenance and prompt repairs will preserve them almost indefinitely. New frames, or frames which have been stripped, should always be treated with a clear wood preserver before they are painted.

Regular maintenance

The bottom rail of a softwood sash is most vulnerable to rot, particularly if it is left unprotected. Rainwater seeps in behind old shrunken putty and moisture is gradually absorbed through cracked or flaking paintwork. Carry out an annual check and deal with any faults. Cut out old putty that has shrunk away from the glass and replace it. Remove flaking paint, make good any cracks in the wood with flexible filler and repaint. Do not forget to paint the underside of the sash.

Replacing a sash rail

Where rot is well advanced and the rail is beyond repair it should be cut out and replaced. This should be done before the rot spreads to the stiles, otherwise you will eventually have to replace the whole sash frame.

Remove the sash by unscrewing the hinges or, if it is a double-hung sash window, by removing the beading.

With a little care the repair can be carried out without removing the glass, though if the window is large it is safer to do so. In any event, cut away the putty from the damaged rail.

The bottom rail is tenoned into the stiles (1), but it can be replaced, using bridle joints. Saw down the shoulder lines of the tenon joints (2) from both faces of the frame and remove the rail.

Make a new rail, or buy a length of moulding if it is a standard section, then mark and cut it to length with a full-width tenon at each end. Set the positions of the tenons to line up with the mortises of the stiles. Cut the shoulders to match the rebated sections of the stiles (3) or, if there is a decorative moulding, pare the moulding from the stile to leave a flat shoulder (4). Cut slots in the ends of the stiles to receive the tenons.

Glue the new rail securely into place with a waterproof resin adhesive and reinforce the two joints with pairs of 6mm (¼in) stopped dowels. Drill the stopped holes from the inside of the frame and stagger them.

When the adhesive is dry, plane the surface as required and treat the new wood with a clear preserver. Reputty the glass and apply paint as soon as the putty is firm.

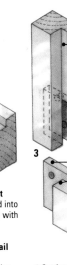

1 The original joint
The rail is tenoned into the stile and fitted with wedges.

2 Cutting out the rail
Saw down the shoulder lines of the joints from both faces of the frame.

STILE
TENON
BOTTOM RAIL
1
2
SHOULDER LINES

STILE REBATE
DOWELS
MITRE
FLAT SHOULDER
SLOTS
3
TENON
SHOULDERS
MITRE
4

3 Cutting the joint
Cut tenons at each end of the rail with the shoulders matching the sections of the stiles.

4 Moulded frames
Pare away the moulding of the stile to receive the square shoulder of the rail. Mitre the moulding.

REPLACING A FIXED-LIGHT RAIL

The frames of some fixed lights (windows) are made like sashes, but are screwed permanently to the jamb and mullion. Such a frame can be repaired in the same way as a sash (see left) after its glass is removed and it is unscrewed from the window frame. Where this proves too difficult you will have to carry out the repair *in situ*.

First remove the putty and the glass, then saw through the rail at each end, close to the stile. Use a chisel to pare away what remains of the rail and chop out the tenons from the stiles. Cut a new length of rail to fit between the stiles and cut housings in its top edge at both ends to take loose tenons (1). Place the housings so that they line up with the mortises and make each housing twice as long as the depth of the mortise.

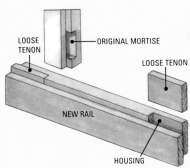

LOOSE TENON — ORIGINAL MORTISE
LOOSE TENON
NEW RAIL
HOUSING

1 Cut housings at each end for loose tenons

Cut two loose tenons to fit the housings and two packing pieces. The latter should have one sloping edge (2).

Apply an exterior woodworking adhesive to all of the jointing surfaces, place the rail between the frame members, insert the loose tenons and push them sideways into the mortises. Drive the packing pieces behind the tenons to lock them in place. When the adhesive has set, trim the top edges, treat the new wood with clear preserver, replace the glass and reputty. Repaint once the putty is firm.

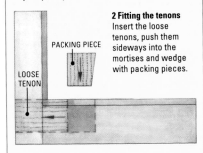

PACKING PIECE
LOOSE TENON

2 Fitting the tenons
Insert the loose tenons, push them sideways into the mortises and wedge with packing pieces.

● **Removing glass**
Removing glass from a window frame in one piece is not easy, so be prepared for it to break. Apply adhesive tape across the glass to bind the pieces together if it should break. Chisel away the putty to leave a clean rebate, then pull out the sprigs. Work the blade of a putty knife into the bedding joint on the inside of the frame to break the grip of the putty. Steady the glass and lift it out when it is freed.

REPAIRING
ROTTEN SILLS

The sill is a fundamental part of a window frame, and if one is afflicted by rot it can mean major repair work.

A casement-window frame is constructed in the same way as a doorframe and can be repaired in a similar way. All the glass should be removed first. The window board may also have to be removed, then refitted level with the replacement sill.

Make sure that the damp-proofing of the joint between the underside of the sill and the wall is maintained. Modern gun-applied mastics have made this particular problem easier to overcome. Some traditional frames have a galvanized-iron water bar between the sill and sub-sill. When replacing a sill of this type without removing the whole frame you may have to discard the bar and rely on mastic sealants to keep the water out.

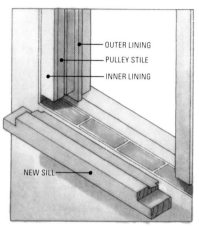

Traditional frame with stone sub-sill

Replacing a wooden sill

Do not simply replace a sill by cutting through it and fitting a new section between the jambs. Even if you seal the joints with mastic, any breakdown of the sealant will allow water to penetrate the brickwork and end grain of the wood, and you may find yourself doing the job all over again.

Serious rot in the sill of a sash window may require the whole frame to be taken out. Make and fit a new sill, using the old one as a pattern. Treat the new wood with a preserver and take the opportunity to treat the old wood which is normally hidden by the brickwork. Apply a bead of mastic sealant to the sill, then replace the complete frame in the opening from inside. Make good the damaged plaster.

It is possible to replace the sill from the inside with the frame in place (see right). Saw through the sill close to the jambs and remove the centre portion. Cut away the bottom ends of the inner lining level with the pulley stiles and remove the ends of the old sill. Cut the ends of the new sill to fit round the outer lining, and under the stiles and inner lining. Fit the sill and nail or screw the stiles to it.

Cut the new sill to fit the frame

Repairing a stone sub-sill

The traditional stone sills that feature in older houses may become eroded by the weather if they are not protected with paint. They are also liable to crack if the wall subsides.

Repair cracks and eroded surfaces with a ready-mixed quick-setting waterproof mortar. Rake out the cracks to clean and enlarge them. Dampen the stone with clean water and work the mortar well into the cracks, finishing flush with the top surface.

Undercut any depressions caused by erosion to help the mortar adhere – a thin layer of mortar simply applied to a shallow depression in the surface will not last for long. Use a cold chisel to cut away the surface of the sill at least 25mm (1in) below the finished level and remove all traces of dust.

Make a wooden former to the shape of the sill and temporarily nail it to the brickwork. Dampen the stone, trowel in the mortar and tamp it level with the former, then smooth it out. Leave the mortar to set for a couple of days before removing the former. Allow it to dry thoroughly before applying paint.

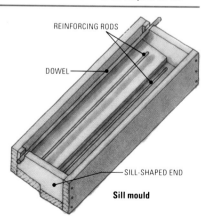

Make a wooden former to the shape of the sill

CASTING A NEW SUB-SILL

Cut out what remains of the old stone sill with a hammer and cold chisel. Make a wooden mould with its end pieces shaped to the same section as the old sill. The open top of the mould represents the underside of the sill.

Fill two-thirds of the mould with fine-aggregate concrete, tamped down well. Add two lengths of mild-steel reinforcing rod, judiciously spaced to share the volume of the sill, then fill the remainder of the mould. Set a narrow piece of wood such as a dowel into notches cut in the ends of the mould. This is to form a 'throat' or drip groove in the underside of the sill.

Cover the concrete with polyethylene sheeting or dampen it regularly for two to three days to prevent rapid drying. When the concrete has set (allow about seven days), remove it from the mould and lay the new sill in the wall on a bed of mortar, packed from underneath with slate to meet the wooden sill.

Sill mould

RE-CORDING A SASH WINDOW

In time, the sash cords from which the sashes are suspended will wear and eventually break. Replace both cords even if only one has broken.
Waxed sash cording is normally sold in standard hanks, although some suppliers sell it by the metre. Each sash requires two lengths of cord, measuring about three-quarters the height of the window. Do not cut it to length beforehand.

Removing the sashes

Lower both sashes and cut through the cords with a knife to release the weights. Hold on to the cords and lower the weights as far as possible before allowing them to drop.

Use a wide-bladed paint scraper to prise off the side staff beads from inside the frame, bending them in the middle until their mitred ends spring out.

Lean the inner sash towards you and mark the ends of the cord grooves on the face of the sash stiles (1). Reposition the sash and carry the marks on to the pulley stiles. The sash can now be pulled clear of the frame.

Carefully prise out the two parting beads from their grooves in the stiles. You can then remove the top sash, after marking the ends of the grooves as before. Place the sashes safely aside.

To gain access to the weights, take out the pocket pieces which were trapped by the parting bead and lift the weights out through the openings.

Pieces of thin wood known as parting strips are usually suspended inside the box stiles to separate each pair of weights. Push the strips aside to reach the outer weights.

Remove the old sash cords from the weights and sashes, and clean up the wood ready for the new cords.

Fitting the sashes

The top sash is fitted first, but not before all the sash cords and weights are in place. Clean away any build-up of paint from the pulleys. Tie a length of fine string to one end of the hank of sash cording. Weight the other end of the string with small nuts or a piece of chain. Thread the weight, known as a mouse, over a pulley (2) and pull the string through the pocket opening until the cord is pulled through. Attach the end of the cord to the weight with a special knot (see below left).

Pull on the cord to hoist the weight up to the pulley, then let it drop back about 100mm (4in). Hold it temporarily in this position with a nail driven into the stile just below the pulley. Cut the cord level with the mark on the pulley stile (3). Repeat this procedure for the cord on the other side, and similarly for the bottom sash.

Replace the top sash on the sill, lean it towards you and locate its cords in the grooves in the stiles. Nail the cords in place, using three or four 25mm (1in) round wire nails. Nail only the bottom 150mm (6in), not all the way up (4). Lift the sash to check that the weights do not touch bottom.

Replace the pocket pieces and pin the parting beads in their grooves. Fit the bottom sash in the same way. Finally replace the staff beads, taking care to position them accurately or you may trap the bottom sash.

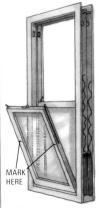

The workings of a double-hung sash window

1 Pulleys	**5** Parting bead
2 Bottom sash	**6** Bottom-sash weight
3 Staff bead	**7** Pocket
4 Top sash	**8** Top-sash weight

HOW TO TIE A SASH-WEIGHT KNOT

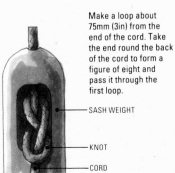

Make a loop about 75mm (3in) from the end of the cord. Take the end round the back of the cord to form a figure of eight and pass it through the first loop.

SASH WEIGHT

KNOT

CORD

MARK HERE

1 Mark cord grooves

STRING

CORD

MOUSE

2 Pull cord through

CUT HERE

3 Cut cords at mark

NAIL HERE

4 Nail cord to sash

SPIRAL
BALANCES

Spiral-balance components
Each balance consists of a torsion spring and a spiral rod housed in a tube. The top end is fixed to the frame stile and the inner spiral to the bottom of the sash. The complete unit can be housed in a groove in the sash stile or in the window frame.

Fixing plate for horned sash.

TUBE

SPIRAL

FIXING PLATE

A spiral-balance unit

Fit top-limit stop

Fit bottom-limit stop

Instead of counterweights and cords, modern sash windows use spiral balances which are mounted on the faces of the frame stiles, eliminating the need for traditional box frames. Pairs of balances are made to match the size and weight of individual glazed sashes and can be ordered through builders' merchants or by post from the manufacturers.

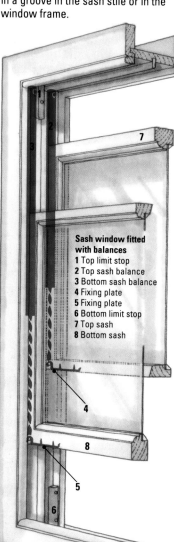

Sash window fitted with balances
1 Top limit stop
2 Top sash balance
3 Bottom sash balance
4 Fixing plate
5 Fixing plate
6 Bottom limit stop
7 Top sash
8 Bottom sash

You can fit spiral sash balances to replace the weights in a traditionally constructed sash window.

Remove the sashes and weigh them on your bathroom scales. Place your order, giving the weight of each sash together with its height and width, plus the height of the window frame. Refit the sashes temporarily until the balances arrive, then take them out again and remove the pulleys.

Plug the holes and paint the box-frame stiles. Cut grooves, as specified by the manufacturers, in the stiles of each sash to take the balances (**1**). Also cut a housing at each end of their bottom edges to receive the spiral-rod fixing plates. Fit the fixing plates with screws (**2**).

Sit the top sash in place, resting it on the sill, and fit the parting bead. Take the top pair of balances, which are shorter than those for the bottom sash, and locate each in its groove (**3**). Fix the top ends of the balance tubes to the frame stiles with the screw nails provided (**4**) and set the ends tight against the head.

Lift the sash to its full height and prop it with a length of wood. Hook the wire 'key' provided by the makers into the hole in the end of each spiral rod and pull each one down about 150mm (6in). Keeping the tension on the spring, add three to five turns anti-clockwise (**5**). Locate the end of each rod in its fixing plate and test the balance of the sash. If it drops, add another turn on the springs until it is perfectly balanced. Take care not to overwind the balances.

Fit the bottom sash in the same way, refitting the staff bead to hold it in place. Fit the stops that limit the full travel of the sashes in their respective tracks (see far left).

RENOVATING
SPIRAL BALANCES

In time the springs of spiral balances may weaken. Re-tension them by unhooking the spiral rods from their fixing plates, then turn the rods anti-clockwise once or twice.

The mechanisms can be serviced by releasing the tension and unwinding the rods from the tubes. Wipe them clean and apply a little thin oil, then rewind the rods back into the tubes and tension them as described above.

1 Cut a groove in the sash stiles

2 Fix the plates in their housing with screws

3 Fit the sash and locate the tube in its groove

4 Nail the top end of the tube to the stile

5 Tension the springs with the key provided

READY-MADE WINDOWS

Joinery suppliers offer a range of ready-made window frames in both hardwood and softwood. Some typical examples are shown below.

Manufactured wooden frames are treated with preserver and some are ready-primed for painting or prestained for final finishing. With the increased awareness of energy conservation, most frames are rebated to take double-glazed sealed units as well as traditional single glazing.

In addition to the stays and fasteners supplied with the frames, some windows also have the top rail of the opening sash, or the frame itself, slotted to take a ventilator kit to comply with Building Regulations for background ventilation in habitable rooms.

Self-assembly kits composed of machined framing are available to make frames of any size to fit non-standard window openings.

Casement windows

Vertical sliding sash windows

The style of the windows is important to the appearance of any house. If you are replacing windows in an older dwelling it is preferable – and not necessarily more expensive – to have new wooden frames made to measure rather than change to modern windows of aluminium or plastic.

Planning and Building Regulations

Window conversions do not normally need planning permission as they come under the heading of house improvement or home maintenance, but if you plan to alter your windows significantly – for example by bricking one up or making a new window opening, or both – you should consult your local Building Control Officer.

All authorities require minimum levels of ventilation to be provided in the habitable rooms of a house, and this normally means that the openable part of windows must have an area at least one-twentieth that of the room. Also, part if not all of a top vent must be 1.75m (5ft 9in) above the floor. Trickle ventilators with a 4000mm^2 (6½ sq in) opening are also required for new installations.

If you live in a listed building or in a conservation area, you should also check with your local authority before making any changes to your windows.

Buying replacement windows

Try to maintain the character of an older house by preserving the original joinery. If you have to replace the window, copy the original style – specialist joinery firms will make up wooden frames to fit. Specify an appropriate hardwood or, for a painted finish, softwood impregnated with a timber preserver.

Alternatively, you can approach a replacement-window company, though this is likely to limit your choice to aluminium or plastic frames. Ready-glazed units can be fitted to your old timber sub-frames or to new hardwood ones supplied by the installer. Most replacement-window companies also fit the windows they supply, and their service includes disposing of the old windows and debris.

This method saves time and effort, but you should carefully consider the compatibility of such windows with the style of your house. Choose a frame that reproduces the proportions and method of opening of the original window as closely as possible.

Replacing a casement window

Measure the width and height of the window opening. If the replacement window needs a timber sub-frame (and the existing one is in good condition), take your measurements from inside the frame. Otherwise, take them from the brickwork. You may have to cut away some of the rendering or internal plaster first in order to obtain accurate measurements. Order your replacement window accordingly.

Remove the old window by first taking out the sashes and then the panes of glass in any fixed light. Unscrew exposed fixings, such as may be found in a metal frame, or chisel away the plaster or rendering and cut through the fixings with a hacksaw. It should be possible to knock the frame out in one piece, but if not, saw through it in several places and lever the pieces out with a crowbar (**1**). Clean up the exposed brickwork with a bolster chisel to make a neat opening.

1 Lever out the pieces of the old frame

Cut the horns off the new frame, then wedge the frame in the window opening and check it is plumb (**2**). Drill screw holes through the stiles into the brickwork (**3**), then remove the frame and plug the holes or use frame fixings. Attach a bituminous-felt damp-proof course to the jambs and sill and refit the frame, checking again that it is plumb before screwing it firmly in place.

Make good the wall with mortar and plaster. Gaps of 6mm (¼in) or less can be filled with mastic. Glaze the new frame as required.

2 Fit the new frame   **3 Drill fixing holes**

REPLACEMENT WINDOWS

Joining frames
A flexible sealant is used for joining standard frames. The frames are screwed together to fit the opening.

Bay windows

A bay window is a combination of window frames built out from the face of the building. The side frames may be set at 90- or 45-degree angles to the front of the house. Curved bays are also made with equal-sized frames set at a very slight angle to each other to form a faceted curve.

The brick structure that supports the window frames may continue up through all storeys, finishing with a gable roof. Alternatively, the bay might have a brick base only, or be supported on brackets, with a flat or pitched roof.

Bay windows can break away from the main wall as a result of subsidence caused by poor foundations or differential ground movements. Damage from slight movement can be repaired once it has stabilized by repointing the brickwork and applying mastic sealant to gaps round the woodwork. However, any damage from extensive or persistent movement should be dealt with by a builder. Consult your local Building Control Officer and inform your insurance company.

Fitting the frame
Where the height of the original window permits, fit standard window frames to make up a replacement window. Various combinations of frames can be joined with shaped hardwood corner posts to set the side frames at an angle of 90 or 45 degrees. A sealant is used to weatherproof the joints between the posts and frames.

90-degree-angle bay

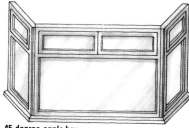

45-degree-angle bay

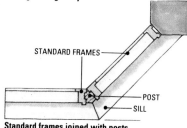

STANDARD FRAMES

POST
SILL

Standard frames joined with posts

Modern angled bay with decorative lead flashing

Bow windows

These windows are constructed on a shallow curve and normally project from a flat wall. Complete hardwood bow-window frames are available from joinery suppliers, ready for installation in a brickwork opening. A flat-topped canopy of moulded plastic is made for finishing the top of the window in place of a traditional lead-sheet covering.

Fitting the frame
Tack damp-proof-course material to the sides of the frame and the underside of the sill, then fit both the frame and the canopy into the wall opening, the outer edges of the frame set flush with the wall. Screw the frame to the brickwork. The vertical damp proofing should overlap any damp-proof course built into the wall.

Weatherproof the canopy with a lead flashing cut into the wall and dressed over the upturned rear edge of the canopy. Use mastic to seal the joints between the frame and the brickwork.

Attractive bow window that suits an older house

REPLACING A SASH WINDOW

Traditional boxed-sash windows fitted with cords and counterweights can be home-made or supplied by specialists who can also fit them for you. Alternatively, an old vertically sliding sash window can be replaced with a new frame with spiral-balance sashes.

Remove the sashes, then take out the old frame from inside the room. Prise off the architrave, then the window boards, and chop away the plaster as necessary. Most frames are wedged in their openings, and you can loosen one by simply hitting the sill on the outside with a heavy hammer and a wood block. Lift out the frame (1) and remove any debris from the opening.

Fit a traditional sash-window frame

exactly like the original, making sure the wood is treated with preserver.

Set a new spring-balance type (which has a thinner frame) centrally in the window opening. Check the frame for plumb and wedge the corners at the head and sill. Make up the space left by the old box stiles with mortared brickwork (2).

Metal brackets screwed to the new frame's jambs can also be set in the mortar joints to secure the frame.

When the mortar has set, replaster the interior wall and replace the architrave. Glaze the sashes and apply a mastic sealant to the joints between the exterior brickwork and the frame to keep rainwater out.

1 Lift out old frame

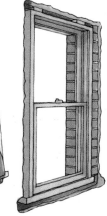

2 Fill gaps with brick

SEE ALSO

Details for:
Plasterboard   40-41

Double-glazed roof windows are becoming increasingly popular for the modernizing of old attic skylights and as part of a loft conversion. They are supplied ready-glazed and fully equipped with catches and ventilators. Flashing kits to fit the frame and to suit high-profile or low-profile roofing material are also available.

Centre-pivoting sashes can be used for roofs with pitches between 15 and 90 degrees. Top-hung windows are available for pitched roofs between 15 and 75 degrees. A combined top-hung and central-pivot variant is also available to provide a large opening that can be used as an emergency exit.

Roof windows are relatively easy to fit, using ordinary woodworking tools. They can usually be installed from inside the roof space and the glass can be cleaned conveniently from inside. Accessories such as remote-opening devices and blinds are also available.

Roof windows used in a traditional building

Internal and external blinds are available

Choosing the size

Cost is always a consideration when choosing roof windows, but take into consideration also the total area of glass that will be necessary to provide a suitable level of daylight in the room. The manufacturers of roof windows offer a standard range of sizes.

The height of the window is also quite important and is largely determined by the pitch of the roof. Manufacturers produce charts which give the recommended dimensions according to roof pitch. Ideally, if the window is to provide a reasonable outlook, the bottom rail should not obstruct the view from normal seat height, nor should it cut across the line of sight of someone standing. Broadly speaking, this means that the shallower the pitch of the roof, the taller the window needs to be. However, the top of the window should always remain within comfortable reach.

Standard-size windows can be set side-by-side or placed one above the other to create a larger window; the widest single window available measures 1.34m (4ft 4¼in). When deciding on the size of a window, bear in mind its proportions and position in relation to the building's appearance.

You probably will not need planning permission to install this type of window, but check if you live in a listed building or in a conservation area. However, the structural alterations will require Building Regulations approval, and so will a complete loft conversion.

The manufacturers of roof windows supply fixing instructions to suit installation in all situations. Below is a summary of one type of window fitted in a slate-covered roof. The frame for a tiled roof has a different flashing kit.

Fitting a window

Start by stripping off the roof covering material over the area which is to be occupied by the window. The final placing of the frame will be determined by the position of the rafters and the roofing. Start by setting the bottom of the window frame at the specified distance above the nearest full course of slates and try to position it so as to have half or whole slates on each side.

Cut through the slating battens, roofing felt and rafters to make the opening, following the dimensions that are given by the manufacturer. Cut and nail horizontal trimmers between the rafters to set the height of the opening, and a vertical trimmer or trimmers to set the width.

With the glazed sash removed, screw the window frame in place with the brackets provided. A guideline is clearly marked round the frame, and you must set this level with the surface of the roofing battens. Check that the frame is square by measuring across its diagonals to be sure they are equal.

Complete the outside work by fitting the slates and flashing kit, working up from the bottom of the frame. Replace the glazed sash.

Cut and nail plasterboard to the sides of the rafters on the inside and close the top and bottom of the opening with plasterboard nailed in the groove provided in the frame and to the timbers of the roof structure.

Finish off the joints with filler and tape, ready for decoration.

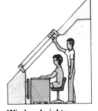

Window height
The height should enable someone sitting or standing to see out of the window with ease.

Lining the opening with plasterboard
Section through a window seen from the inside, showing the lining on the side, top and bottom of the opening. Prefabricated linings are also available.

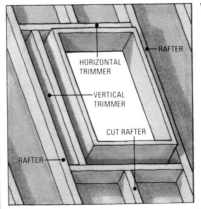

HORIZONTAL TRIMMER

VERTICAL TRIMMER

RAFTER

CUT RAFTER

RAFTER

Cut the opening and fit trimmers

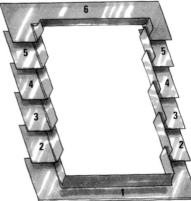

Flashing kit showing order of assembly

BUILDING
TOOLS

Using a pointing hawk
A pointing hawk
makes the filling of
mortar joints very
easy. Place the lip of
the hawk just under a
horizontal joint and
scrape the mortar into
place with a jointer.

**Continental-pattern
trowels**

● **Essential tools**
Brick trowel
Pointing trowel
Plasterer's trowel
Mortar board
Hawk
Spirit level
Try square
Plumb line

76

BUILDER'S TOOL KIT

A specialist builder – such as a
plasterer, joiner or bricklayer –
needs only a limited set of tools,
whereas the amateur is more
like a one-man general builder,
who has to be able to tackle all
kinds of construction and repair
work, and therefore requires a
much wider range of tools than
the specialist.

The tool kit suggested here is
for renovating and improving
the structure of your home and
for such tasks as erecting or
restoring garden structures and
laying paving. Electrical work,
decorating and plumbing call for
other sets of tools.

FLOATS AND TROWELS

*For a professional builder, floats
and trowels have their specific
uses – but in home maintenance
a repointing trowel may often be
the ideal tool for patching small
areas of plaster, or a plasterer's
trowel for smoothing concrete.*

London-pattern trowel

Canadian-pattern trowel

Brick trowels
A brick trowel is for handling
and placing mortar when laying
bricks or concrete blocks. A
professional might use one with
a blade as long as 300mm (1ft)
– but such a trowel is too heavy
and unwieldy for the amateur, so
buy a good-quality brick trowel
with a fairly short blade.

The blade of a **London-pattern
trowel** has one curved edge for
cutting bricks, a skill that takes
much practice to perfect; the
blade's other edge is straight, for
picking up mortar. This type of
trowel is made in right-handed
and left-handed versions, so be
sure to buy the right one for you.
A right-handed trowel has its
curved edge on the right when
you are holding the tool.

A **Canadian-pattern trowel**
is symmetrical, so it's convenient
when people with different left-
hand and right-hand preferences
want to share the one trowel.

Pointing trowel
A pointing trowel is designed for
repairing or shaping mortar joints
between bricks. The blade is only
75 to 100mm (3 to 4in) long.

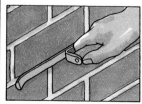

Jointer
Use a jointer to shape the mortar
joints between bricks. Its narrow
blade is dragged along the
mortar joint and the curved front
end used for shaping the
verticals.

Frenchman
A Frenchman is a specialized tool
for scraping off excess mortar
from brickwork jointing. You can
make one by heating and bending
an old table knife or a metal strip.

Wooden float
A wooden builder's float is for
applying and smoothing cement
renderings and concrete to a
fine, attractive texture. The more
expensive ones have detachable
handles, so their wooden blades
can be replaced when they wear.
Similar floats made from plastic
are also available.

Plasterer's trowel
A plasterer's trowel is a steel
float for applying plaster and
cement renderings to walls. It is
also dampened and used for
'polishing', stroking the surface
of the material when it has
firmed up. Some builders prefer
to apply rendering with a heavy
trowel and finish it with a more
flexible blade – but one has
to be quite skilled to exploit such
subtle differences.

BOARDS FOR CARRYING
MORTAR OR PLASTER

Any convenient-sized sheet of
12 or 18mm (½ or ¾in) exterior-
grade plywood can be used as
a mixing board for plaster or
mortar. A panel about 1m (3ft)
square makes an ideal mixing
board, while a smaller spotboard, about 600mm (2ft) square,
is convenient for carrying the
material to the actual work site.
Screwing some battens to the
underside of the boards makes
them easier to lift and carry.

You will also need a small
lightweight hawk for carrying
pointing mortar or plaster. Make
one by nailing a block of wood
underneath a plywood board so
you can plug a handle into it.

A home-made hawk

LEVELLING AND MEASURING
TOOLS

*You can make some levelling
and measuring tools yourself –
but don't skimp on essentials,
such as a good spirit level and
a robust tape measure.*

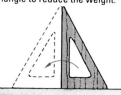

VIAL

Spirit level
A spirit level is a machine-made
straightedge incorporating
special glass tubes or vials that
contain a liquid. In each vial an
air bubble floats. When a bubble
rests exactly between two lines
marked on the glass, then the
structure on which the level is
held is known to be properly
horizontal or vertical, depending
on the orientation of the vial.

Buy a wooden or lightweight
aluminium level, 600 to 900mm
(2 to 3ft) long. A well-made one
is very strong, but treat it with
care and always clean mortar or
plaster from it before they set.

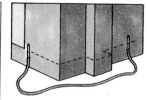

Water level
You can make a water level by
plugging short lengths of trans-
parent plastic tubing into the
two ends of a garden hose; fill
the hose with water till it appears
in both tubes. Since water level
remains constant, the levels
in the tubes are always identical
and can therefore be used for
marking identical heights, even
over long distances and round
obstacles and bends.

Builder's square
A large set square is useful when
you set out brick or concrete-
block corners. The best squares
are stamped out of sheet metal,
but you can make a serviceable
one by cutting out a thick plywood right-angled triangle with
a hypotenuse of about 750mm
(2ft 6in). Cut out the centre of the
triangle to reduce the weight.

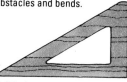

Checking a square
*Accuracy is important, so check
the square by placing it against a
straight batten on the floor. Draw
a line against the square to make
a right angle with the batten,
then flop the square to see if it
forms the same angle from the
other side.*

Try square
Use a try square for marking out
square cuts or joints on timber.

Making a plumb line
*Any small heavy weight hung on
a length of fine string can act as
a plumb line for judging whether
a structure or surface is vertical.*

BUILDING

TOOLS

Bricklayer's line

This is a nylon line used as a guide for laying bricks or blocks level. It is stretched between two flat-bladed pins that are driven into vertical joints at the ends of a wall, or between line blocks that hook over the bricks at the ends of a course. As a substitute, you can stretch string between two stakes driven into the ground outside the line of the wall.

Steel pins and line

Buy the special flat-bladed pins, or make your own by hammering flats on 100mm (4in) nails.

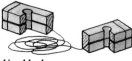

Line blocks

The blocks grip the corners of the bricks at the end of a course; the line passes through their slots.

Plasterer's rule

This is simply a straight length of wood used for scraping plaster and rendering undercoats level.

Straightedge

Any length of straight rigid timber can be used to check whether a surface is flat, or (in conjunction with a spirit level) to see whether two points are at the same height.

Gauge stick

For gauging the height of brick courses, calibrate a softwood batten by making sawcuts across it at 75mm (3in) intervals – which is the thickness of a brick plus its mortar joint.

Tape measure

An ordinary retractable steel tape measure is adequate for most purposes; but if you need to mark out or measure a large plot, hire a wind-up tape – which can be up to 30m (100ft) in length.

Marking gauge

A marking gauge has a sharp steel point for scoring a line on timber parallel to the edge. Its adjustable stock acts as a fence and keeps the point a constant distance from the edge.

Several types of hammer are useful on a building site.

Claw hammer

Choose a strong claw hammer for building stud partitions, nailing floorboards, making doorframes and window frames, and putting up garden fencing.

Club hammer

A heavy club hammer is used for driving cold chisels and for a variety of demolition jobs. It is also useful for driving large masonry nails into walls.

Sledgehammer

Hire a sledgehammer if you have to break up hardcore or paving. It's also the best tool for driving stakes or fence posts into the ground, though you can make do with a club hammer if the ground is not too hard.

Mallet

A carpenter's wooden mallet is the proper tool for driving a wood chisel. But you can use a hammer instead if the chisel has an impact-resistant plastic handle.

SAWS

Every builder needs a range of handsaws, but consider hiring a power saw when you have to cut a lot of heavy structural timbers – especially if you plan to rip floorboards down to width, which is a very tiring job when done by hand.

Special saws are available for cutting metal, and even for sawing through masonry.

Panel saw

All kinds of man-made building boards are used in house construction, so it is worth investing in a good panel saw.

It can also be used for cutting large structural timbers to the required lengths.

Tenon saw

This is a good saw for accurately cutting wall studs, floorboards, panelling and joints. The metal stiffening along the top of the blade keeps it rigid and prevents the saw from wandering off line.

Padsaw

Also called a keyhole saw, this small saw has a narrow tapered blade for cutting holes in timber.

Coping saw

A coping saw has a frame that holds a fairly coarse but very narrow blade under tension for cutting curves in wood.

Floorboard saw

If you prise a floorboard above its neighbours, you can cut across it with an ordinary tenon saw – but the curved cutting edge of a floorboard saw makes it easier to avoid damaging the boards on either side.

Hacksaw

The hardened-steel blades of a hacksaw have fine teeth for cutting metal. Use one to cut steel concrete-reinforcing rods or small pieces of sheet metal.

Sheet saw

A hacksaw's frame prevents its use for cutting large metal sheets – but a sheet saw has a replaceable hacksaw blade bolted to the edge of a flat blade that can pass through the sheet like a handsaw. It will also cut corrugated plastic sheeting and roofing slates.

Universal saw

A universal or general-purpose saw is able to cut wood, metal, plastics and building boards. The short frameless blade has a low-friction coating.

This type of saw is particularly useful for cutting secondhand timber, which may contain nails or screws that would blunt the blade of an ordinary woodsaw.

POWER SAWS

A *circular saw* will accurately rip timber or man-made boards down to size. As well as saving you the effort of hand-sawing large timbers, a sharp power saw produces such a clean cut that there is often no need for planing afterwards.

A *power jigsaw* is able to cut curves in timber and boards. It is equally useful for cutting holes in fixed wall panels and for sawing through floorboards.

A *reciprocating saw* is a two-handed power saw that has a long pointed blade. It is powerful enough to saw sections of heavy timber, and can even cut through a complete stud partition.

Masonry saw

Masonry saws closely resemble handsaws for wood, but their tungsten-carbide teeth cut brick, concrete blocks and stone.

DRILLS

A powerful electric drill is invaluable to a builder. A cordless version is useful when you have to bore holes outdoors or in lofts and cellars that lack convenient electric sockets.

Power drill

Buy a good-quality power drill, plus a range of twist drills and spade or power-bore bits for drilling timber. Make sure the drill has a percussion or hammer action for drilling walls. For masonry you need special drill bits tipped with tungsten carbide. The smaller ones are matched to the size of standard wall plugs; there are also much larger ones that have reduced shanks, so they can be used in a standard power-drill chuck. The larger bits are expensive, so it pays to hire them. Percussion bits are even tougher than masonry bits, and have shatter-proof tips.

Brace

A brace is the ideal hand tool for drilling large holes in timber. In addition, when fitted with a screwdriver bit, it provides the necessary leverage for inserting or extracting large woodscrews.

Drilling masonry for wall plugs

Set the drill to hammer action and low speed. Wrap tape round the bit to mark the depth to be drilled, allowing for slightly more depth than the length of the plug, as dust will pack down into the hole as the plug is inserted. Drill the hole in stages, partly withdrawing the bit at times in order to clear the debris.

To protect paintwork and floorcoverings from falling dust, tape a paper bag just below the position of the hole before starting drilling.

● **Essential tools**
  Straightedge
  Tape measure
  Claw hammer
  Club hammer
  Panel saw
  Tenon saw
  Hacksaw
  Padsaw
  Power drill
  Masonry bits
  Brace and bits

GLOSSARY
OF TERMS

Architrave
The moulding around a door or window.

Bolster
A wide-bladed cold chisel for cutting bricks and concrete blocks. It is also useful for levering up floorboards.

Casing
The timber lining of a door opening.

Cavity wall
A wall of two separate masonry skins with an air-space between them.

Chase
A groove cut in masonry or plaster to accept pipework or electrical cable. *or* To cut such grooves.

Cold chisel
A solid-metal octagonal-section chisel used to cut a chase in masonry.

Cornice
The horizontal moulding between walls and ceiling.

Coving
A prefabricated moulding used to make a cornice.

Dado
The lower part of an interior wall – usually defined with a moulded rail.

Damp-proof course – DPC
A layer of impervious material which prevents moisture rising from the ground into the walls of a building.

Damp-proof membrane – DPM
A layer of impervious material which prevents moisture rising through a concrete floor.

Dovetail nailing
A jointing technique, using two nails driven at opposing angles to fix one piece of wood to another.

Efflorescence
A white powdery deposit caused by soluble salts migrating to the surface of a wall or ceiling.

End grain
The surface of wood exposed after cutting across the fibres.

Flashing
A weatherproof junction between a roof and a wall or chimney, or between one roof and another.

Footing
A narrow concrete foundation for a wall.

Furring battens
See Furring strips.

Furring strips
Parallel strips of wood fixed to a wall or ceiling to provide a framework for attaching panels.

Grounds
Strips of wood fixed to a wall to provide nail-fixing points for skirting boards and door casings. *See also* Pallet.

Head plate
The top horizontal member of a stud partition.

Heave
An upward swelling of the ground caused by excess moisture.

Horns
Extended door or window stiles that protect the corners while in storage.

Jamb
The vertical side member of a door or window frame.

Joist
A horizontal wooden or metal beam used to support a structure like a floor, ceiling or wall.

Key
To abrade or incise a surface to provide a better grip when gluing something to it.

Lath and plaster
A method of finishing a timber-framed wall or ceiling. Narrow strips of wood are nailed to the studs or joists to provide a supporting framework for plaster.

Lintel
The horizontal beam that supports the wall over a door or window opening.

Mastic
A non-setting compound used to seal joints.

Mullion
A vertical dividing member of a window frame.

Muntin
A central vertical member of a panel door.

Needle
A wooden beam used with props to support the wall above an opening prior to the installation of an RSJ or lintel.

Nogging
A short horizontal wooden member between studs.

Nominal sizes
The standard sizes of sawn timber. Even planed timber is specified by nominal sizes because planed dimensions are not uniform.

Pallet
A wooden plug built into masonry to provide a fixing point for a door casing.

Party wall
The shared wall between two houses and over which each of the adjoining owners has equal rights.

Pinch rod
A batten used to gauge the width of a door casing.

Reveal
The vertical side of an opening in a wall.

Rolled steel joist – RSJ
A steel beam, usually with a cross section in the form of a letter I.

Sash
The openable part of a window.

Scratchcoat
The bottom layer of cement render.

Screed
A thin layer of mortar applied to give a smooth surface to concrete etc.

Screed batten
A thin strip of wood fixed to a surface as a guide to the thickness of an application of plaster or render.

Scribe
To copy the profile of a surface on the edge of sheet material which is to be butted against it. *or* To mark a line with a pointed tool.

Sill
The lowest horizontal member of a stud partition. *or* The lowest horizontal member of a doorframe or window frame.

Sleeper wall
A low masonry wall used as an intermediate support for ground-floor joists.

Sole plate
Another term for a stud-partition sill. *or* A wooden member used as a base to level a timber-framed loadbearing wall.

Staff bead
The innermost strip of timber holding a sliding sash in a window frame.

Stile
A vertical side member of a door or window sash.

Stretcher bond
A form of brick bonding where the vertical joints are staggered by 50 per cent.

Stud partition
An interior timber-framed dividing wall.

Studs
The vertical members of a timber-framed wall.

Subsidence
A sinking of the ground caused by the shrinkage of excessively dry soil.

Transom
A horizontal dividing member of a window frame.

Vapour barrier
A layer of material which prevents the passage of moisture-laden air.

Vapour check
See Vapour barrier.

Wall flanges
Metal flanges that clip onto each side of an electrical mounting box. The flanges fit behind a plasterboard wall lining, gripping it between them and the socket or switch faceplate.

Wall plate
A horizontal timber member placed along the top of a wall to support joists and to spread their load.